SPANISH TRAILS
A guide to walking in the Spanish mountains

THE MOUNTAINS OF MADRID

BOOK THREE OF A SERIES

PHIL LAWLER
TIM PRICE

First Edition published 2020 by
Spanish Steps,
Skipton
North Yorkshire

Copyright © Phil Lawler
The right of Phil Lawler to be identified as the author
of this work has been asserted by him in accordance with the
Copyright, Designs and Patents Act 1988

All rights reserved. This book is sold subject to the condition that no part of this book is to be reproduced, in any shape or form. Or by way of trade, stored in a retrieval system or transmitted in any form or by any means, electronic, mechanical, photocopying, recording, be lent, re-sold, hired out or otherwise circulated in any form of binding or cover other than that in which it is published and without a similar condition, including this condition being imposed on the subsequent purchaser, without prior permission of the copyright holder.

Disclaimer

The author has taken all reasonable effort to ensure that the information herein is accurate, however the author accepts no responsibility if it is not, nor if unforeseen circumstances occur while doing the routes. We would also advise that in planning your route you check local transport, accommodation and please be aware that some paths and rights of way may be affected by changes such as development or weather. We would appreciate any information regarding changes. You can do this by contacting the Publisher in the first instance.

Photographs and Maps © 2020 Phil Lawler and Tim Price

The author has his own website: http://www.spanishtrailsco.com

Production by 2QT Limited (Publishing), Settle, North Yorkshire
Cover design by Charlotte Mouncey (using authors' photograph)

Printed in Great Britain by
TJ Books Limited

A CIP catalogue record for this book is available
from the British Library

ISBN 978-0-9955797-2-9

La Mujer Muerta - **WALKS 7 & 11**

DISCLAIMER

The walk descriptions and maps in this publication are as accurate as I can make them, but things change and I cannot guarantee that everything is always up to date or 100% correct. You must take all reasonable precautions, wearing adequate clothing, carrying waterproofs, mobile phone and so on, just as you would when hill walking in the UK. You also need protection from the sun. And let somebody know where you are going when you set out.

All users of this information use it entirely at their own risk.

ABOUT THE AUTHORS

PHIL LAWLER

Phil Lawler spent his formative years walking the Yorkshire Dales. In later years, his job took him to live in Madrid. He worked in most of Spain's larger cities, and he got to know the country anfd its mountains intimately. In the process, he got to understand Spanish culture and gained a fluent command of the language.

Having left his 'proper' job in Madrid, Phil spent several years leading walking groups in different parts of the country. Now retired, he still walks in Spain, principally in the Picos de Europa, the Sierra Guadarrama, Cazorla and the Sierra Almijara, but also in the Pyrenees, Somiedo and other parts.

If you enjoy what he has written here and need more information, you are welcome to contact him on: info@spanishtrailsco.com.

TIM PRICE

Although British, Tim is Madrid born and bred; walking in La Pedriza with his father is among his earliest childhood memories. He has known Phil since the 90s when they both lived in the city.

Tim now lives in Becerril de la Sierra – at the foot of the Guadarrama range – and is very knowledgeable of the area. Indeed, he spends much of his spare time (he still has a 'proper' job) running and walking in the mountains described in this book, as well as in many other parts of Spain.

Ibex in La Pedriza - **WALKS 26 & 27**

CONTENTS

DISCLAIMER 3
ABOUT THE AUTHORS 4
ACKNOWLEDGEMENTS 11
INDEX TO THE WALKS 13
ABOUT SPANISH TRAILS 18
THE MOUNTAINS OF MADRID 19

WALK NO. 1
LAS MACHOTAS 32

WALK NO. 2
SIERRA DE MALAGON 37

WALK NO. 3
ABANTOS AND SAN JUAN 43

WALK NO. 4
CUEVA VALIENTE 49

WALK NO. 5
CERRO DE SALAMANCA FROM ALTO DEL LEON 55

WALK NO. 6
LA PEÑOTA 61

WALK NO. 7
LA MUJER MUERTA FROM ORTIGOSA DEL MONTE (SEGOVIA) 66

WALK NO. 8
SIERRA DE QUINTANAR 71

WALK NO. 9
CERRO DEL AGUILA AND PEÑA BERCIAL 75

WALK NO. 10
MONTON DE TRIGO ... 80

WALK NO.11
LA MUJER MUERTA FROM LAS DEHESAS (CERCEDILLA) ... 85

WALK NO. 12
MIRADOR LUIS ROSALES AND MAJALASNA ... 89

WALK NO. 13
LOS SIETE PICOS (THE SEVEN PEAKS) ... 95

WALK NO. 14
PUERTO DE FUENFRIA AND SENDA HERREROS ... 100

WALK NO. 15
MIRADOR DE LAS CANCHAS ... 105

WALK NO. 15a
MIRADOR DE LAS CANCHAS AND PEÑA PINTADA ... 108

WALK NO. 16
BOLA DEL MUNDO, LA MALICIOSA AND FUENTE DE LA CAMPANILLA ... 111

WALK NO. 17
LA BARRANCA TO LA MALICIOSA VIA CUERDA DE LAS BUITERERAS ... 115

WALK NO. 18
ASCENT OF LA MALICIOSA (2,227 metres) FROM BECERRIL DE LA SIERRA ... 123

WALK NO. 19
SIERRA DE LOS PORRONES AND CHARCA VERDE ... 128

WALK NO. 20
PEÑALARA AND THE CINCO LAGUNAS ... 137

WALK NO. 21
REVENTON ... 143

WALK NO. 22
LA BOLA DEL MUNDO AND THE WESTERN CUERDA LARGA ... 147

WALK NO. 23
CABEZAS DE HIERRO ... 155

WALK NO. 24
LA NAJARRA AND ASOMATE DE HOYOS FROM PUERTO DE LA MORCUERA ... 162

WALK NO. 25
MIRAFLORES TO LA NAJARRA AND PICO PERDIGUERA ... 166

WALK NO. 26
LA PEDRIZA AND EL YELMO ... 173

WALK NO. 27
LAS TORRES DE LA PEDRIZA ... 179

WALK NO. 28
HUECO DE SAN BLAS AND LA PEDRIZA ... 185

WALK NO. 29
MONDALINDO AND PEÑA NEGRA ... 191

WALK NO. 30
PATONES DE ARRIBA TO CANCHO DE LA CABEZA ... 197

WALK NO. 31
LA CABRERA CIRCUIT ... 204

Riscos de Cancho Negro

ACKNOWLEDGEMENTS

Phil wishes to thank most of all Tim Price, his co-author for this edition, without whom it would have been impossible to complete it.

He also owes thanks to many people for their support for his work in various parts of Spain, in particular:

- Jane
- Sue and Gordon at Hotel Finca el Cerrillo in Andalucia
- Manuel and Carmen at Hotel Peña Castil in Sotres
- Pedro and Maite at Hostal Corona in Posada de Valdeon
- Annette, Allan and others for their companionship on many of the walks

La Pedriza from La Maliciosa peak

INDEX TO THE WALKS

WALK NO.	ROUTE	DISTANCE (kms)	ASCENT (metres)
1 - Moderate	Las Machotas	16	800

DESCRIPTION: *Two summits near El Escorial*

2 - Easy	Sierra de Malagon	13	750

DESCRIPTION: *A pleasant walk from San Lorenzo to a cross overlooking the town*

3 - Moderate or Strenuous	Abantos and San Juan	12 or 19	900 or 1,200

DESCRIPTION: *Ascent to one or more summits on the GR10 long-distance path*

4 - Strenuous	Cueva Valiente	20	950

DESCRIPTION: *Ascent to a summit from the northern side of the sierra, and along the broad Carrasqueta ridge*

5 - Easy	Cerro de Salamanca from Puerto del Leon	11.5	500

DESCRIPTION: *A walk to three tops along the GR10*

6 - Strenuous	La Peñota	17	1010

DESCRIPTION: *A prominent summit on the GR10 and a visit to a remote monument*

7 - Very Strenuous	La Mujer Muerta from the north side	25	1275

DESCRIPTION: *A walk to three summits along a major ridge*

INDEX TO THE WALKS

8 - Moderate	Sierra de Quintanar	16	980

DESCRIPTION: *The western continuation of the Mujer Muerta ridge*

9 - Moderate	Cerro del Aguila and Peña Bercial	19	995

DESCRIPTION: *A circuit from Las Dehesas to three intermediate summits*

10 - Easy	Monton de Trigo	12	803

DESCRIPTION: *Ascent to an intermediate but very distinctive well-known summit*

11 - Strenuous	La Mujer Muerta from Las Dehesas	21	1205

DESCRIPTION: *The traverse of this well-known ridge by its classic route*

12 - Moderate to Strenuous	Mirador Luis Rosales and Majalasna	16	850

DESCRIPTION: *A circuit to two viewpoints and the lowest of the Siete Picos (Seven Peaks)*

13 - Easy	Los Siete Picos (the Seven Peaks)	11	570

DESCRIPTION: *A popular walk on an easy path, ascending to traverse six of the seven peaks on a prominent granite ridge*

14 - Strenuous	Puerto de Fuenfria and Senda Herreros	16.5	650

DESCRIPTION: *A circuit along easy and then more difficult paths on increasingly rough terrain*

| 15 - Easy | Mirador de las Canchas | 10 | 390 |

DESCRIPTION: *An easy walk through Scots pine woods to a wonderful viewpoint*

| 15a - Moderate | Mirador de las Canchas and Peña Pintada | 14 | 680 |

DESCRIPTION: *As walk 15 but ascending to traverse a high, broad ridge*

| 16 - Strenuous | Bola del Mundo, La Maliciosa and Fuente Campanilla | 14 | 950 |

DESCRIPTION: *A spectacular walk to two high peaks returning at lower level with great views*

| 17 - Strenuous | La Maliciosa via Cuerda de las Buitreras | 12 or 15 | 900 or 1050 |

DESCRIPTION: *An ascent to the great peak of La Maliciosa via a little-used route*

| 18 - Strenuous | La Maliciosa from Becerril de la Sierra | 14 | 1170 |

DESCRIPTION: *A direct ascent to this major peak from the edge of the town of Becerril de la Sierra*

| 19 - Very Strenuous | Sierra de los Porrones and Charca Verde | 24 | 1200 |

DESCRIPTION: *An ascent towards La Maliciosa from the east, along a prominent ridge, and with an optional and avoidable ascent on metal pins*

| 20 - Strenuous | Peñalara and the Cinco Lagunas (Five Lakes) | 15 | 860 |

DESCRIPTION: *An ascent to the highest point in the Sierra de Guadarrama*

21 - Strenuous	Reventon	24	1270

DESCRIPTION: *A circular walk from San Ildefonso along a broad ridge. Graded strenuous due to distance rather than terrain*

22 - Strenuous or very Strenuous	Bola de Mundo and the western Cuerda Larga	12 or 24	900 or 1500

DESCRIPTION: *A long and demanding ascent on a an unconventional route, but with a shorter version if required*

23 - Strenuous	Cabezas de Hierro	23	1200

DESCRIPTION: *A walk to the highest part of the Cuerda Larga ridge*

24 - Moderate	La Najarra and Asomate de Hoyos	14	800

DESCRIPTION: *An ascent to and traverse of the eastern part of the Cuerda Larga*

25 - Strenuous	La Najarra and Pico Perdiguera	26	1350

DESCRIPTION: *Ascent to two eastern summits from the town of Miraflores de la Sierra*

26 - Strenuous	La Pedriza and El Yelmo	17	870

DESCRIPTION: *A walk into the granite national park of La Pedriza, visiting the elephant rock (El Elefantito) and the base of El Yelmo*

| 27 - Strenuous | Las Torres de la Pedriza | 17 | 1200 |

DESCRIPTION: *An ascent to the highest point in La Pedriza, through remote and rugged granite landscape*

| 28 - Strenuous | Hueco de San Blas and La Pedriza | 24 | 1370 |

DESCRIPTION: *A circuit on the eastern flanks of La Pedriza, with boulder scrambling and reaching the Cuerda Larga*

| 29 - Moderate | Mondalindo and Peña Negra | 21 | 1050 |

DESCRIPTION: *A walk to two rounded peaks to the eastern end of the Sierra de Guadarrama*

| 30 - Moderate | Patones de Arriba to Cancho la Cabeza | 15 | 910 |

DESCRIPTION: *A circuit from an interesting, formerly-abandoned village, with views over a reservoir*

| 31 - Moderate | La Cabrera | 17 | 650 |

DESCRIPTION: *A circuit of a spectacular granite ridge with an optional ascent to the summit*

ABOUT SPANISH TRAILS

This is Book Three of the series Spanish Trails, providing walks in the hills to the north of the city of Madrid, mainly but not exclusively within the Sierra de Guadarrama.

Book One of the series covers the Picos de Europa in the north of Spain, and Book Two provides walks in the mountains near Competa and Nerja in the south of the country.

In principle the books are for hill walkers rather than strollers. However, the walks are graded from easy to very strenuous, and hopefully there will be something here for everybody.

Publications in the series:

Spanish Trails Book One – Los Picos de Europa.
ISBN 978-0-9955797-0-5

Spanish Trails Book Two – Sierra Almijara and Tejeda.
ISBN 978-0-9955797-1-2

Spanish Trails Book Three – the Mountains of Madrid.
ISBN 978-0-9955797-2-9

www.spanishtrailsco.com

THE MOUNTAINS OF MADRID

AN INTRODUCTION

Madrid is the capital city of Spain, but it is also the administrative capital of the Comunidad de Madrid (the community or province of Madrid). The city's population is about 3.3 million, but another 3 million or more live in the province, which includes several smaller cities, such as Alcala de Henares to the east, Fuenlabrada and Mostoles to the south, and Alcobendas to the north. Together, these form a major metropolitan area. But less than 50 kilometres from the city centre are the magnificent mountains of the Sierra de Guadarrama, rising to an altitude of 2,428 metres above sea level, some 1,700 metres higher than the city centre. The hills are visible from the northern area of the city, and as a result of their proximity to Madrid, they make a popular hill-walking and skiing area.

Although Madrid can be exceptionally hot in the summer months (temperatures can exceed 40 degrees in the shade) the winter weather can be cold and snow is normal at higher levels. There are ski resorts (with short pistes) at Valdesqui and Puerto de Navacerrada. These places also make good centres for walking, and are included in the walks in this collection.

Most of the walks described here are in the Sierra de Guadarrama, the range which forms a line going roughly from El Escorial in the north-west to La Cabrera in the north-east. We have also included walks which are not strictly speaking in the Guadarrama, and one or two are partly outside Madrid province. But they are complementary to the others, and provide a comprehensive exploration of the high land to the north of Madrid.

One area of particular note is La Pedriza, which is near Manzanares el Real, and in the Regional Park of the Alto Manzanares. It is full of enormous rock formations and unusual granite shapes surrounding the Manzanares river. Many of the rocks have names, such as the *Elefantito* (Little Elephant) and the *Tortuga* (Tortoise). You can invent your own names as you explore the area.

CENTRES OF POPULATION

The walks are close to the following towns or centres:

To the north-west – El Escorial; Guadarrama; Cercedilla; Navacerrada; Puerto de Navacerrada; Mataelpino and San Ildefonso /La Granja.

To the north – Manzanares el Real; Miraflores de la Sierra and Soto del Real.

To the north-east – La Cabrera; Torrelaguna and Bustarviejo.

HOW TO GET THERE

Madrid Airport is situated to the east of the city. There is good public transport to the city centre by bus or metro. There are two main rail hubs in the centre. Atocha serves the south of the country (although the high-speed Alta Velocidad Española (AVE) also leaves here for the north, e.g. Barcelona), and Chamartin serves the north in general.

From Chamartin there are direct trains on the Cercanias (local) network to El Escorial and Cercedilla (Line C-8) in the foothills of the mountains. From Cercedilla there is a light railway (Line C-9) to the pass Puerto de Navacerrada and on to Cotos, close to the highest peak in the area, Peñalara.

Also from Chamartin there are direct Cercanias trains (Line C-4B) to Colmenar Viejo, which is not directly in the mountains, but from where there are bus services to Manzanares el Real and the spectacular mountain area of La Pedriza. There is also a direct Cercanias train to El Escorial and there is an hourly service to Segovia.

Buses go from Madrid to more or less all the walking areas, departing from the bus station at La Moncloa, or perhaps better from Plaza Castilla in the north of the city centre. At the time of writing, lines 664, 684, 691 and 724 are some of the more useful routes.

Timetables are on https://www.redtransporte.com/madrid/autobuses-interurbanos.

If you are driving from the airport, look for the M40 ring road going towards Burgos. The following three roads lead north from the M40: * the A1 north, signposted to Burgos, will lead you to the north-eastern walking areas, such as La Cabrera and Patones; * the M607 goes north to Colmenar Viejo and on to Cercedilla and Navacerrada. *and from the M607, near Colmenar Viejo a right fork takes you on to the M609 to Manzanares el Real.

All of these places are accessible on good quality roads from Madrid and from the airport. You will need to obtain more details with a road map and/or satnav.

At busy times (e.g. Sundays and bank holidays), there are vehicular access restrictions to La Pedriza. Also Las Dehesas can be congested. Further information is given, along with the specific walks affected.

ADVICE

In winter you are likely to encounter snow in the hills. At the start of the year there is usually sufficient for skiing. If you go walking in the winter, pay attention to the weather forecasts, and in January to March or even early April, you may need snow shoes to get to the higher levels. On the exposed sections, such as los Riscos on Peñalara, you may need crampons, and in fact it can be dangerous in such places, so take advice from the visitor centres before starting out.

However, from the time of snow melt (about late April) onwards, all the walks in this collection can be done with normal hill-walking equipment. Good walking shoes or boots are required, along with waterproofs and layers of light clothing. Walking poles are always an advantage, and a mobile phone is nowadays a 'must'. The international emergency number is 112. Only use it in a genuine emergency, and if necessary say "English" and you will be provided with help.

Always carry supplies of food in case of emergency, and take plenty of water, as supplies in the hills are very limited and in some cases non-existent.

There is a lot of wildlife here. The animal you are most likely to see is the cabra montesa, a member of the ibex family, which is endemic to the Iberian Peninsula and is very common in the Guadarrama. In La Pedriza they are accustomed to meeting human beings and may even approach you. They can be large animals, and I always take care not to disturb them, especially the large males when they are guarding the herd. I have never known one to attack a human being. They are more likely to attack each other, I think.

There are snakes, which can be poisonous, but they don't want to meet you any more than you want to meet them. But if you see one give it a wide berth and leave it alone. There are processional caterpillars on pine trees. They make cocoon-style nests in trees, and both caterpillar and nest can cause severe rashes and allergic reactions on contact due to fine hairs containing a toxin. Special care should be taken with dogs and children to ensure that they do not ingest anything covered in the hairs. So, again, just leave them alone and do not handle them. They are prevalent in the spring.

The birdlife in the hills is predominantly vultures and eagles, which can be spectacular and normally present no problems for walkers.

THE WALKS

The walks include easy walks, more difficult ones, some strenuous ones, and in just one or two cases a degree of exposure. These mountains are granite, and are generally broad ridges and rounded summits. So in most cases there is no significant exposure, but where there is, this is indicated in the walk descriptions.

The walks are arranged in a sequence broadly speaking covering the whole range of the Guadarrama and nearby places, starting in the west at El Escorial and ending in the east at Patones. The focal point is the Madrid region, but in many cases the routes follow the ridge line which forms the border between the Madrid region and the Comunidad of Castilla y Leon, and more specifically the province of Segovia.

Some of the walks actually start and end in Segovia province, but in each case they cross the border line into Madrid. Because of this, anybody doing these walks will have the opportunity to visit the city of Segovia as well as that of Madrid. Both are well worth a diversion or even a journey.

The key landmarks in the area are Peñalara (the highest peak); La Maliciosa (perhaps the most prominent peak); La Cabrera (a magnificent range of hills right at the side of the main N1 Madrid/Burgos motorway); and La Pedriza. The latter is a labyrinth of shattered granite rocks, with lots of great walking. It would be very easy to get lost here, but it is well worth exploring and this book contains several routes in that area.

There are some popular centres for starting and finishing walks. They are well placed for accessing certain areas of the mountains, and they are provided with parking spaces. These include the towns of San Lorenzo del Escorial and Manzanares el Real, and also the public car parking areas at

Las Dehesas and la Barranca. In each of those cases several walks will commence at the same place, and in some cases they may cover some of the same ground, but often in the opposite direction, and always so as to provide a different walk overall.

WAYMARKING

Spain has a waymarking system, in which some (but by no means all) paths are numbered and marked with colours.

Paths can be classed as *Gran Recorrido* 'GR' (which means long distance) or *Pequeño Recorrido* 'PR' (short distance).

GR routes are marked with occasional red and white marks on rocks, trees, etcetera. PR routes are similarly marked, but with yellow and white.

The colour-coding system is applied nationally, but the numbering is regional. So, for instance, in the Madrid region a short-distance path may be numbered 'PRM1', 'PRM2', and so on. The long-distance path GR10 crosses the region from east to west, and several of these walks follow parts of this path.

Although the system is at times very helpful, it can be confusing where there are two or more PR routes in close proximity. In this book, we mention the coloured marks and sometimes the route number, where we think this may be helpful. But the routes in this book stand alone. They may follow the GR or PR routes at times and not at others. Although the coloured marks may help you to find the way, the walk descriptions in the book are intended to be self-explanatory, and in the case of a conflict between a paint mark and the walk description, the latter takes precedence.

To make matters even more confusing, in addition to the official PR and GR marks, there are many local routes which have been marked either by a local authority or by an unknown hand. Once again, if in doubt, keep to the instructions in these walk descriptions.

Finally, it helps if you understand the symbols in use on the GR and PR paths. Two horizontal lines mean that the path goes straight ahead. Two lines in a kind of lopsided V-shape going left mean that the path turns left, and vice versa. Where the two colours form a cross, this means that this is the wrong way for that particular route, but only for that particular route. Once again, if you are using this book, it is always the walk description in the book which prevails.

MAPS

The walks in this book include sketch maps showing just the key information you should need to find your way. They should be used in conjunction with one or other of the topographical maps available (see below). Various map references are included at the end of each walk description, and they are cross-referenced by numbers in the sketch maps.

Spanish topographical mapping does not meet the standards of the British Ordnance Survey. There is no single source of good mapping. You have to shop around to see what is available. There is a good selection of maps in the Madrid shop Tienda Verde, and there is a much more limited selection in some of the local shops in the smaller towns of the area. To follow these walks, ideally you should use one of the commercially available maps in conjunction with the sketch maps included here with each walk.

We have not discovered a 25000:1 map which covers the whole of the area covered by this book. But there are lots of maps covering one part or another. You will find them on websites such as Stanfords and Amazon.

We use the following maps, which we believe to be as good as any:

25000:1 – Guadarrama/La Pedriza published by Editorial Alpina. A set of two maps covering the central part of the area covered by this book. ISBN 978-84-8090-566-4

25000:1 – Sierra de Guadarrama published by the government's Centro Nacional de Información Geográfica. A set of two maps covering the central part of the area covered by this book. ISBN 978-84-4164-858-6

50000:1 – Sierra de Guadarrama Parque Nacional published by Desnivel. A smaller scale than the above, but covering a wider area, including El Escorial to the west.

50000:1 – Sierra Norte published by La Tienda Verde. Covers the northern and eastern parts of the area, including Reventón, Mondalindo, La Cabrera and Patones de Arriba.

TERMINOLOGY

Spanish	English
Puerto	Mountain pass

Cerro	Hill
Loma	Hillside or bank
Mirador	Viewpoint
Río	River or stream
Fuente	Spring, usually with a tap (untreated hill water)
Refugio	Mountain refuge
Sendero or Senda	Footpath
Cruz	Cross
Collado	Col (a pass between two hills)

SYMBOLS USED IN THE SKETCH MAPS

Surfaced Road	═══
Dirt Road/Track	-- -- -- --
Footpath	- - - - -
Summit	⋀
Gate	⊢⊣
Signpost	↱
Fuente (Water)	F
Civil War Remains	☆

THE MOUNTAINS OF MADRID

SKETCH MAP OF WALK LOCATIONS

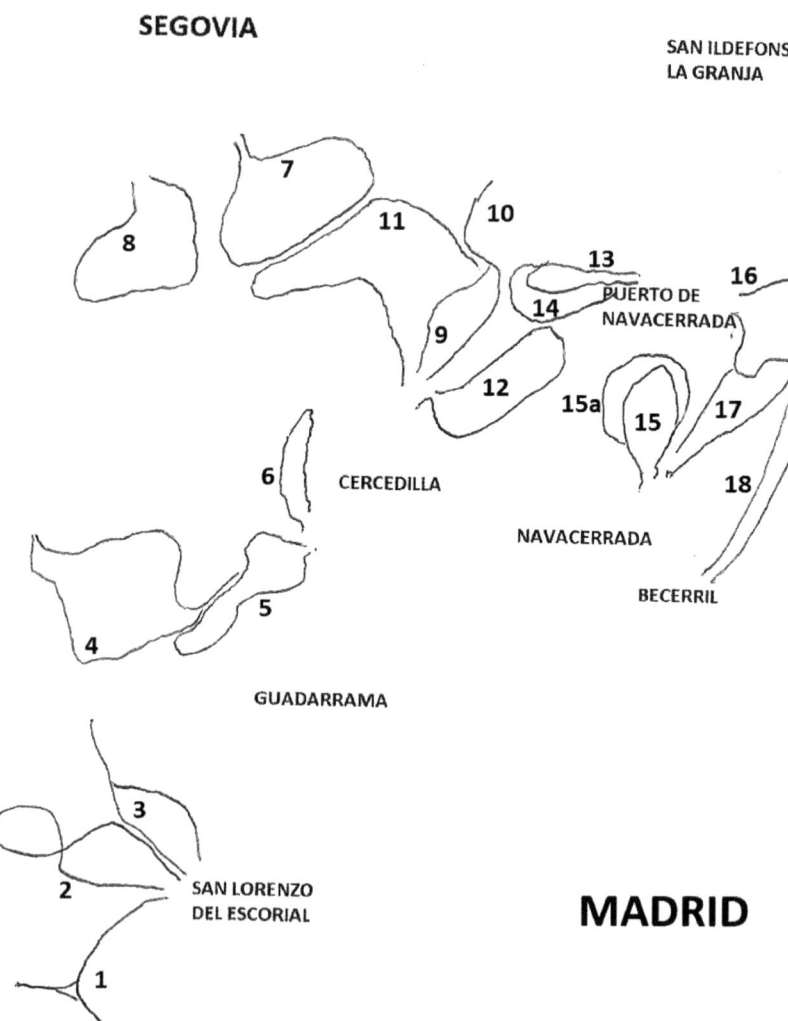

The walk numbers relate to the numbers in the index

Not to scale: *it is just intended to show the location of each walk in relation to each of the others*

PHIL LAWLER

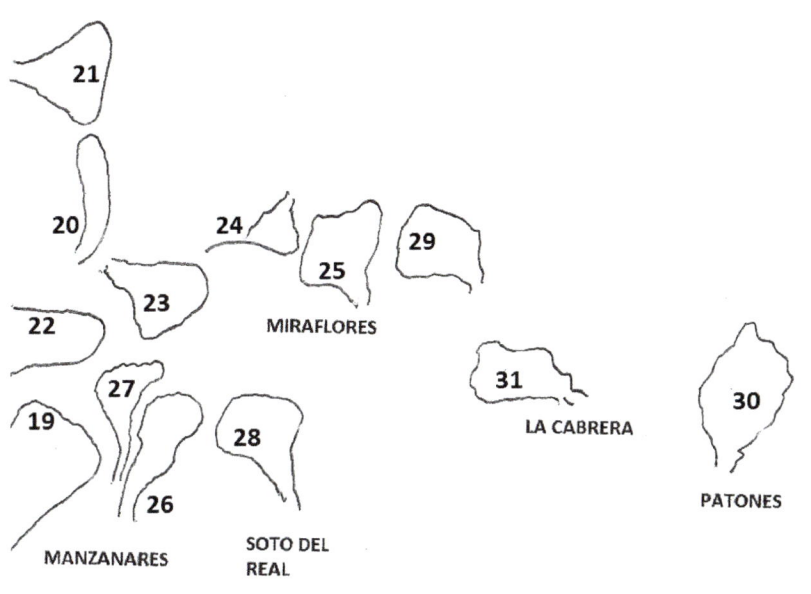

La Najarra Refuge - **WALK 24**

Walks 1 to 3 all begin at the town of San Lorenzo del Escorial. (Note: not the nearby town El Escorial.) Arriving at San Lorenzo, you can hardly miss the enormous monastery. Each of these three walks starts at the door on the northern side of the monastery, which is the exit for people who have toured the interior.

In the town there are public indoor car parks, one of which is next to the bus station. Also, going down the road to the east from the monastery, there are side streets with ample parking.

The monastery of Saint Lawrence was also the 16th century palace of King Felipe II of Spain, who married Mary Tudor in 1554 and sent the Spanish Armada to England in 1588. So, apart from being a beautiful and enormous complex, this place has an interesting history. It is a major tourist attraction, housing many works of art, and in the basement is the pantheon of Spanish royalty. However, this is a walking guide book, so you can study the history elsewhere. But it is well worth the fee of a few euros to make a visit while you are in the area.

LAS MACHOTAS

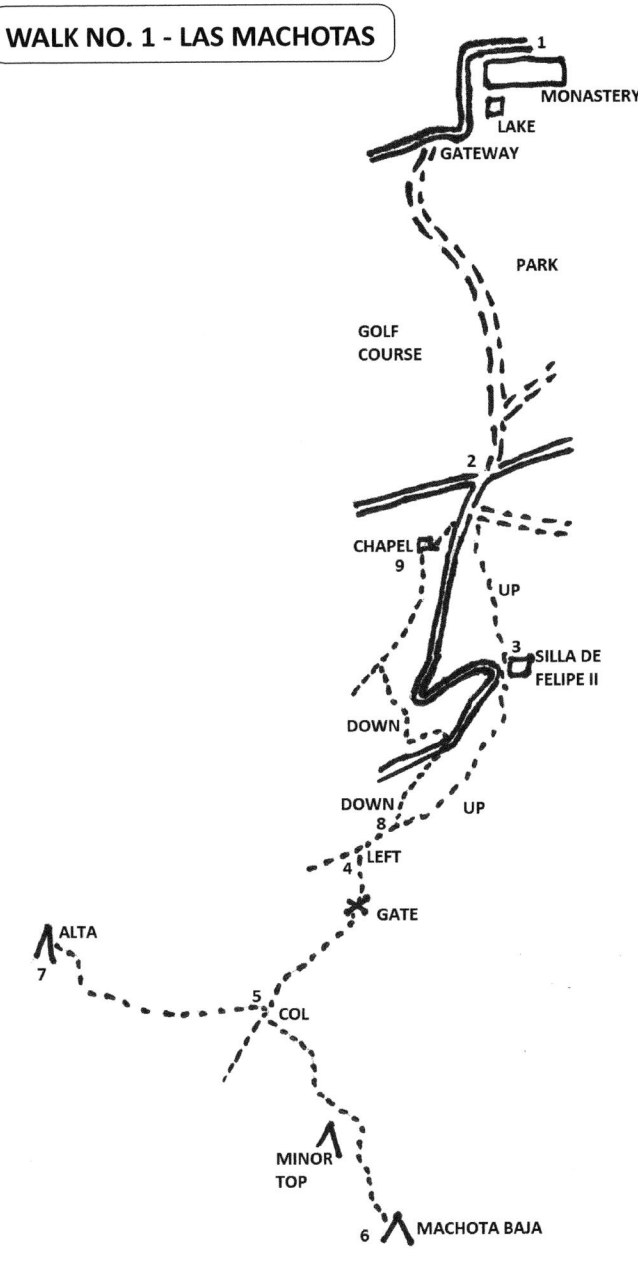

WALK NO. 1

LAS MACHOTAS

Distance	16 km
Ascent	800 metres
Overall grade	Moderate
Terrain	Good footpaths. Some boulder scrambling, but only at the very summit
Exposure	None, subject to the above
Highest point	1,451 metres

The ascent of two relatively easy summits to the southwest of the famous Royal Monastery of San Lorenzo del Escorial. The first summit post sits on top of a granite outcrop. Reaching it involves an awkward scramble onto a large granite boulder, but it is a great walk even if you do not do the final scramble. The second and higher summit is a granite pinnacle. Our objective is to get to its base.

- With your back to the northern door of the monastery *(1)* turn left and walk round the corner to the western side. Walk diagonally across the square to its far corner. Follow the street through some arches. On your left you can go through a doorway to visit a part of the gardens before continuing along the street, with a great view of the monastery and a reservoir on your left. Follow the street to the right and at the next corner turn left into a park. Go to the south across the park. There are several minor footpaths here as well as a broader track. Take whichever you like, but keep going south and then slightly south-west. There is a golf club over to your right (west) and it is fenced, so just stay outside the fence.

- 1.5 kilometres from where you entered the park, cross a road *(2)*. It can be busy so take care. On the far side, a minor road goes gradually uphill to reach the viewpoint at Silla de Felipe II (Felipe II's Seat). But you do not need to walk on the road. 140 metres from entering the park, another track goes to the left (east). Turn left on to this track but immediately leave it, and walk in a southerly direction over the grassy area between this track and the major road. Shortly you will see some sort of fence posts (with no fence) and you can follow them uphill. There is no single correct path here, but keep going south and uphill for 700 metres from leaving the road.
- The paths will lead you to the Silla de Felipe II, a granite outcrop with steps cut into it, making a wonderful viewpoint back on to the town *(3)*. Legend has it that the king sat here to watch the construction of the monastery. It can be busy here, especially at weekends, and there is a café which opens at busy times. From the viewpoint go south, ignore the road going off to the right, and follow a track which soon narrows to a footpath. It is marked with the red and white paint indicating that it is part of the long-distance route GR10.
- For the next part of the walk you can follow the red and white marks. The path veers to the south-west, climbing steadily. At one point, to the right side of a wall, you will see another path going back and down to the right *(8)*. That will be your return route, but for now keep straight on. About 200 metres farther on, the correct route goes sharp left across a wall which has been lowered for this purpose. Take this left turn *(4)* and 300 metres later go through a gate on the right. The path, still the GR10, continues upwards for about another three quarters of a kilometre, to reach a delightful green col (Collado de Entrecabezas) from where the path begins to descend to the south-west.

WALK NO. 1

This col is between the two summits, La Machota Baja (lower) and La Machota Alta (higher).

- On reaching the col *(5)*, turn left. There are footpaths and cattle tracks here. Take any of the tracks going uphill to the south-east. Beyond the first incline you should see a more definitive path heading up towards higher ground. Follow this path, ascending over some loose and stony ground, and then passing below and to the left side of a hilltop. The main summit is ahead on the next hill. You should hopefully be able to discern the summit post ahead. Once more, there is more than one path to the top. Take any path into the col between the two hills, and then go towards the higher top. There are one or two slightly awkward steps over bare rock if you are on higher ground, so you may prefer to stay at a lower level until you get close to the final hill, La Machota Baja.

- Walk up to the summit plateau, where you will find extensive blocks of granite. The summit post *(6)* is on the very top of a large boulder. It is not easy at first to see the post, and it is even less easy to get up to it. If there are two or more of you to help each other, it will be easier. There are two ways up this rock. One is marked vaguely with red paint. The other is round the south side and unmarked. If you manage to get up there take care getting down again because the rock is smooth and there are few handholds.

- From the summit, return via the outward route to the Entrecabezas col *(5)* on the GR10 and go straight across it, passing through a gate by a wall. A path follows the line of the wall more or less all the way (1 kilometre) to the higher summit, La Machota Alta *(7)*. On the summit, there is a rock known as El Fraile, The Monk, due to its resemblance to a monk in his hooded habit.

- Retrace your steps once more via the outward route to the Entrecabezas col *(5)* and turn left back towards La Silla. Follow the GR10 in reverse. You will pass through the gate and then cross the wall *(4)*, turning right on the far side. Then, at a junction of paths, which I mentioned earlier *(8)*, keep left. This nice footpath descends and soon reaches a road. Turn right along it for just 80 metres and then turn left on a path downhill. After 250 metres you will see the road again on your right, but stay on the path straight ahead. After another 250 metres, go to the right on a good path *(9)* until half a kilometre farther on when you will reach a chapel in a meadow, with a *fuente*. From here, follow the minor road north-east to the park entrance, cross the main road and walk back through the park, keeping the golf course to your left and the monastery to your right, to return to the start.

APPROXIMATE GPS WAYPOINTS (UTM)

1	Start	402879 4493890
2	Cross the road	402471 4492257
3	Silla Felipe II	402450 4491468
4	Go left	401840 4490885
5	The col (Entrecabezas)	401352 4490271
6	Machota Baja summit post	401747 4489387
7	Machota Alta	400623 4490695
8	Keep left	401986 4490933
9	Go right	402017 4491540

WALK NO. 2

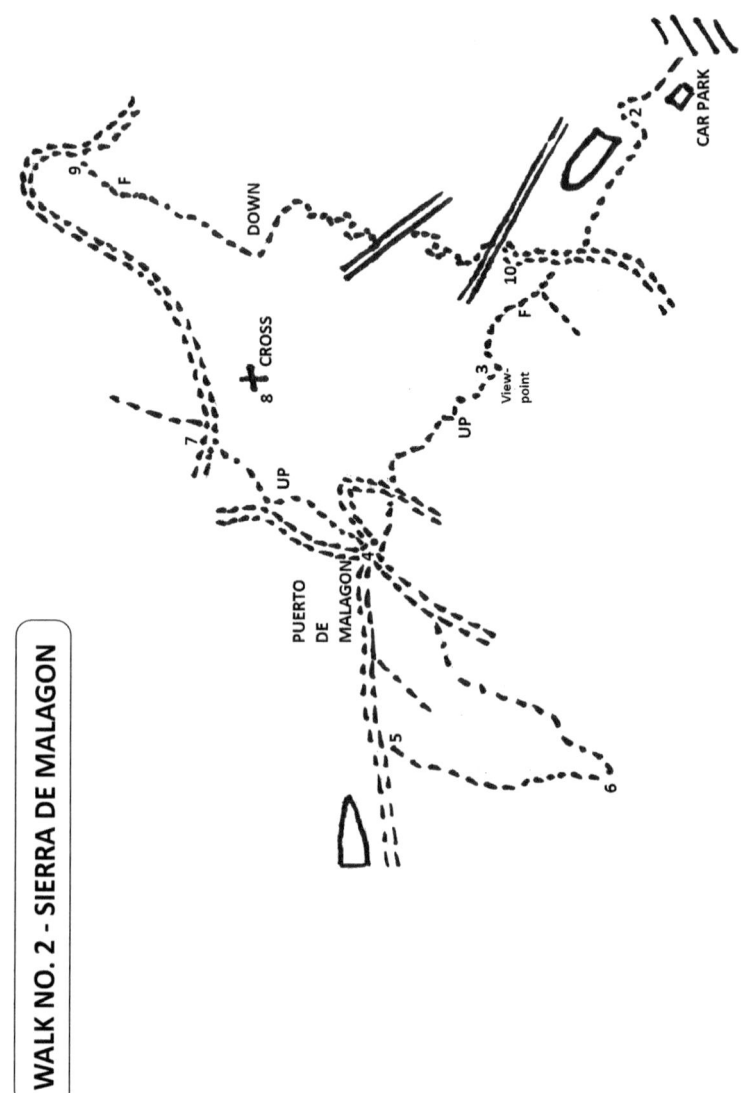

WALK NO. 2 - SIERRA DE MALAGON

WALK NO. 2

SIERRA DE MALAGON

Distance	13 kilometres, plus an optional loop
Ascent	750 metres, excluding the optional loop
Overall grade	Easy
Terrain	Good footpaths and tracks
Exposure	None
Highest point	1,677 metres

A circuit on the hills above San Lorenzo del Escorial, in the area between the Machotas (Walk 1) and Abantos (Walk 3). The route visits the Cruz de Rubens, a cross built on the hillside to the orders of Felipe II and evidently visited later by the famous artists Rubens and Velazquez. Part of this walk, and also part of Walk 3, use the same section of the long-distance route GR10, but in the opposite direction, making for a quite different walk.

The walk begins at the door on the northern side of the monastery of San Lorenzo.

- With your back to the northern door of the monastery *(1)*, go directly across the road and ascend a short steep slope into the town. Turn left at the first street and follow it to the north-west. You will meet some road junctions, but keep going in the same compass direction and find the street named Avenida Carlos Ruiz. It has a car park, but I couldn't describe how to get your car there. So the walk, and my statistics, start from the monastery.

- Once you are on Avenida Carlos Ruiz, walk past the car park on the left. Then as the street swings to the left, look for a path on the right, exactly on the bend *(2)*. Go up the path, and after a very short ascent, swing right. A rough path will lead you past the wall of a dam. Keep going and you should see the water below to your right. At a wire fence, the path veers to the left and uphill. Go through a gate (ensuring that it is closed behind you) and turn right onto a track.

- After only 100 metres a signpost shows a path to the left. Follow this path. It is a *via pecuaria* (a Spanish drove road), and the path is called the Senda de los Tesoros de Abantos. Very soon you will reach a fork where the Tesoros path goes up to the left. But instead take the right fork, which is signposted for a *fuente*. The path passes the *fuente* and continues in zigzags. There are short-cut opportunities but stick to the main path. Cross a minor road, and just to your right the path continues again.

- Keep going uphill, and where the path takes a right turn there is a signpost for a viewpoint, the *Mirador de los Arceles (3)*. It is worth stopping to take in the view. And if you fancy a scramble there are plenty of rocks here to entertain you. But return to the path and continue upwards. Pass a big rocky outcrop on your left and then follow a left and right zigzag. Two minor paths go down to the right to another *fuente*. Ignore them and keep to the main path. At another junction, follow a red arrow straight ahead. You will reach a semi-surfaced road with animal pens on the far side. Cross the road and walk uphill, keeping the pens on your right. You will ascend on a track to some pylons. Just beyond them turn left on a road to reach a gate *(4)* with a view down to the northern side of the sierra and a reservoir in the valley below. This is the Puerto de Malagon (the Malagon Pass).

- *(A ruined building here is the remains of an ice storage house from earlier centuries, marked on some maps as Pozo de la Nieve. At one time there were eight of these in the vicinity of San Lorenzo Monastery. There are others to the north of the summit of Abantos.)*

- From the gate our main route goes to the right (north-east), but for some extra walking and to see some entirely different terrain, you can take the loop which I describe next. If you would like to continue on the shorter, main route, skip this next section.

- To start the extra loop, at Puerto de Malagon go through the gate and walk straight ahead down a broad track going west towards a reservoir in the valley (Embalse de el Tobar). It is pleasant and easy walking. You will pass a path on your left, but my route ignores it and goes on to a second path, about 700 metres from leaving the gate *(5)*. Take this path up to the left. It ascends a slope then starts to descend on the far side of a hill towards some lovely green meadows. I have not seen anybody here, only cattle and horses. Stay on the path for about half a kilometre until you are near a plantation of new trees supported by stakes. You can turn left anywhere here *(6)* and walk across open country, steadily uphill going just south of east. It will bring you to a track near a large *fuente*, where you can turn left. The track will take you back to the gate. When I did this loop it added three easy kilometres distance to the route. I have given a couple of GPS waymarks below.

- As you get near to the gate, look to the hill ahead, to see a white wooden cross on the edge of the hill. That is the Cruz de Rubens, and your next destination. On reaching the gate, go through a turnstile and on to the road, with the gate to your left. Continue on the main route as follows.

- With the gate to your left, take a path to the north-east. It is marked with some green and white paint on a rock at the time of writing. The path passes to the left side of a rocky outcrop, enters woods, and then reaches a road. At this point go to the right, where a minor path goes through a gap between rocks and into the woods. You will soon join a major path. Turn left along it. There is a cairn a few metres further along. Ignore any minor paths and stay on the main one. You will reach a clearing where there is a broken-down wall to the right, and a tall pile of rocks marks a boundary. Keep going on the path until you reach a track where an old signpost tells you all the things you are not allowed to do (lighting fires, etcetera).

- The path crosses the track through a gate *(7)*, but **do not** follow it. Instead, leave the path and turn right along the track. As is starts to swing left, leave the track and walk to the right to reach the white cross *(8)* which is perched above a rocky slope. This is the Cruz de Rubens, a great viewpoint and picnic spot.

- Return from the cross to the track and turn right along it, going north-east. The track heads towards the distant fire lookout building near the summit of Abantos (see Walk no. 3). Stay on the main track until, at the head of a valley on the right, there is a signpost saying 'El Cervonal'. Go just past the sign and then take a footpath down to the right *(9)*. Within a few metres it leads you into a clearing with a *fuente* and red and white marks for the GR10. From now, keep looking for the red and white marks for reassurance, although you are unlikely to lose the trail. At the *fuente*, the path goes down to the right and swings left almost immediately, descending in a fairly straight line through Scots pine trees. Pass a rocky area to the right and the descent steepens. The path now zigzags down until it reaches a road where, at about 10 metres to your left, it continues downhill on the far side of the road.

- The path keeps on zigzagging its way down to reach a turnstile and a gate in a fence. Go through here and down to turn left on a track to a barrier about 30 metres away. Turn right here on a road and follow it round a left-hand bend, to where the GR10 signs show the way through a gate. But do not go that way. Instead, go down to the right *(10)* and cross the stream by another gate. Don't go through the gate, but follow a red arrow up to the left on a broad track. It will soon lead you to the footpath signpost you encountered early in the walk. Go past it. Ignore a turnstile in the fence on your left and continue to the next signpost, where you should turn left and go through the gate (ensuring it closes behind you). The path now takes you down past the dam and back to the street with the car park, from where you can follow your nose back to the town centre and the monastery.

APPROXIMATE GPS WAYPOINTS (UTM)

1	Start and finish	402879 4493890
2	Start of path	402214 4494415
3	Mirador (viewpoint)	401380 4494993
4	Gate	400674 4495482
5	Path on extra loop	400018 4495507
6	Further waypoint on the loop	399799 4494913
7	Track	401091 4496050
8	Cruz de Rubens	401219 4495988
9	Path down	402270 4496704
10	Go right	401886 4494832

WALK NO. 3

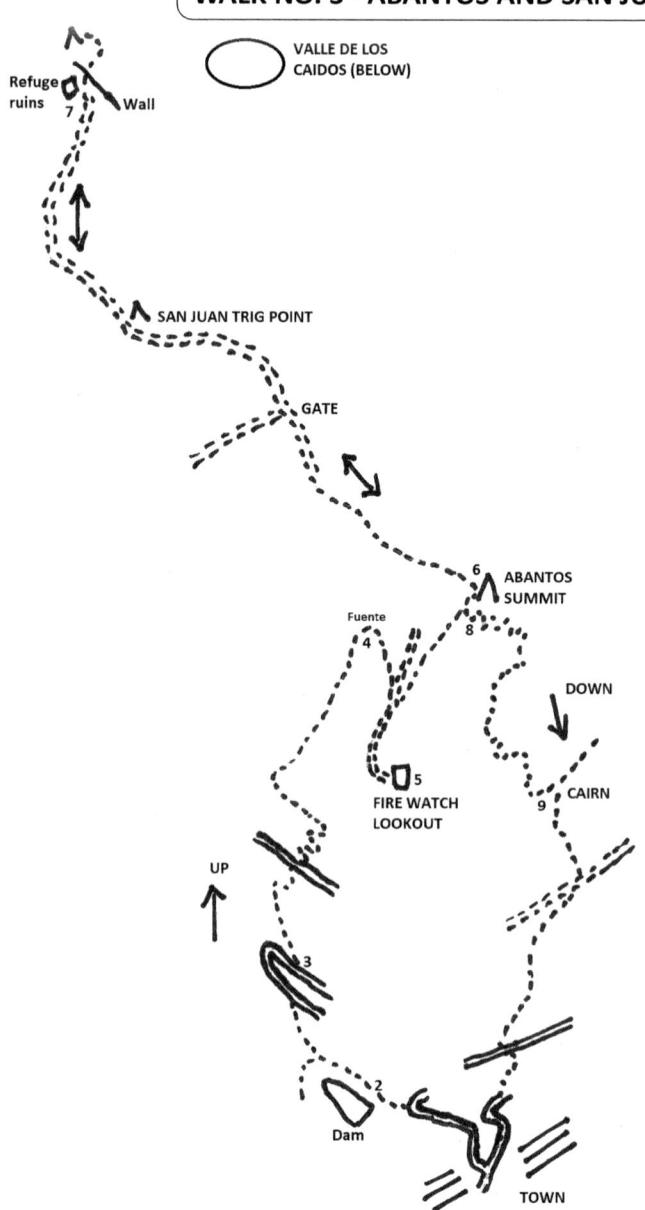

WALK NO. 3

ABANTOS AND SAN JUAN

Distance	19 kilometres – Shorter circuit: 12 kilometres
Ascent	1,200 metres or 900 metres
Overall grade	Strenuous or moderate
Terrain	Good footpaths and tracks
Exposure	None
Highest point	1,750 metres

An ascent to the first two tops on a broad ridge leading north from San Lorenzo del Escorial. The walk starts directly from the monastery of San Lorenzo, follows the long-distance path GR10 to the top of the ridge then leaves it to reach a great viewpoint, from where the summit of Abantos is easily reached.

The shorter circuit returns from the summit following the eastern slopes of the hill. The longer route continues along the ridge for about 3 kilometres to a viewpoint looking down on to the enormous cross of Valle de los Caidos (see notes below), returning to Abantos before the descent.

There are signposts stating that shooting can take place on a Thursday, so take care.

- The walk begins at the northern door of the monastery, exactly as in Walks 1 and 2: with your back to the door *(1)*, cross the road and go up a slope into the town. Turn left and go to the north-western part of the town. Look for a road called 'Carretera de la Presa' (Road to the Dam). Once on this road, follow it round a left-hand bend and uphill. You will pass a signpost for an 'Arboreto' and then reach the dam on your left *(2)*.

- Continue on the road to the side of the dam. If you haven't already seen them, you should start to see red and white markers indicating that you are on the long-distance GR10. When the road swings to the right, continue straight ahead on a footpath. You will very soon find a little path going up to the left, but it just provides a view over the dam. Continue on the main path. Ignore a signpost pointing down to the left to cross the stream, and keep up to the right. You will reach a road/track. Go straight across it and follow the footpath. Go through a green gate, where a sign warns you that hunting is on Thursdays. Once through the gate, continue on the path uphill and slightly to the left.

- Go left along a surfaced road. It quickly swings back to the right. Then very soon, take a sharp turn to the left by a green barrier (which is for traffic, not pedestrians) on to a broad dirt track *(3)*. After about 50 metres, by a red and white marker take a path to the right. It runs parallel with and to the right side of the broad track. Continue uphill on this path until you reach another road. The footpath continues on the far side of the road, just slightly to your left. Higher up you will reach a place where the path goes sharp right and some eroded ground goes straight up over exposed tree roots. You will then pass a rocky area to the left. There is a gradual ascent on a broader track and then the path swings to the right to reach a nice green meadow with a *fuente* in the middle (Fuente Cerbunal) *(4)*. You are still on the GR10 to here, but at the *fuente* you should leave it.

- From the *fuente*, take a path slightly uphill to the right, south-east. It will bring you on to a broad track going south. Follow the track for about half a kilometre until it goes slightly downhill to reach a building on a rocky promontory. It has a gate and a fence. From the top there is a brilliant view back down to the town and monastery. It is, I believe, a lookout post for forest fires, and it makes a terrific viewpoint *(5)*.

- From this viewpoint, return to the north along the same track. After about 350 metres, where the track starts to descend slightly and there are rocks on the right, keep to the high ground on the right and find a minor path along the ridge. It will lead you to the summit of Abantos, where you will find a trig point, a large white cross, and a transmitter with solar panels and a wind-powered generator *(6)*.

- *From here I will describe the longer route. For the shorter route, skip this next section.*

- From the trig point, walk north-west past the transmitter. Do not follow a track downhill to the left. Keep to the high ground to the right. A footpath keeps to the left of a stone wall which runs along the highest part of the broad ridge. Follow the path, which becomes a broader track. About 1.25 kilometres from the summit, you will reach a gate at a junction. Go through the gate and keep straight on. You will pass a trig point at the side of the wall on the right, marking the top of the hill of San Juan (1,740 metres). Then, after a short descent, you will reach a ruined refuge, Refugio de la Naranjera *(7)*. Go past the right side of the ruin and a path leads across the wall towards a large rock outcrop. To the right side of these rocks there is a view directly down to the Valle de los Caidos. You can climb the rocks as far as you are able, but take care here.

- Return the way you came via the refuge, San Juan, the gate, and back to the summit of Abantos.

- From Abantos, take the path you ascended earlier (with the trig point to your left and the transmitter on your right) but after only about 40 metres, at a fork in the path, take the left fork *(8)*. This path is stony, and at first seems quite eroded, but it soon improves, descending the hillside in frequent zigzags. As you descend you will have good views of the San Lorenzo monastery.

- After many zigzags, you will reach a point where the main path goes straight on but a cairn marks the start of a lesser path going back to the right. Turn right at the cairn *(9)*. This path soon improves. It continues down, still in zigzags, to reach a road. Cross the road and the path continues. You will soon have a wall to your right. Keep going to the left side of the wall and descend to reach a road via a green gate. Turn left on the road then take a track down to the right to the top of the town.
- To find your way back to the centre, take the first street to the left, Calle la Anchuela. At the bottom turn right. Go on to the end and turn left down a hill. Turn right into Calle Maria Cristina. Go straight on to the end. At the very end of that street turn right. Steps will lead you down to the town centre.

APPROXIMATE GPS WAYPOINTS (UTM)

1	Start and finish	402879 4493890
2	The Dam	402297 4494521
3	Turn left	401896 4494928
4	Fuente Cerbunal	402245 4496581
5	Viewpoint	402195 4496028
6	Abantos Summit	402649 4496772
7	Refuge (ruined)	400960 4499049
8	Path down	402617 4496763
9	Turn right at cairn	402952 4495883

NOTES: VALLE DE LOS CAIDOS

Valle de los Caidos is officially a monument to the fallen of both sides in the Spanish Civil War (1936 to 1939). It has become highly politicised. A basilica is carved out of the rock underneath the enormous granite cross, which can be seen for miles. Over 30,000 people are buried in the precinct, including the dictator Francisco Franco. Although it was officially a monument to both sides, most of the construction was done by republican prisoners. Franco was buried here, but since he was not one of the fallen, he has recently been re-interred elsewhere. Those loyal to Franco were opposed to this.

Abantos Summit - **WALK 3**

WALK NO. 4 - CUEVA VALIENTE

WALK NO. 4

CUEVA VALIENTE

Distance	20 km
Ascent	950 metres
Overall grade	Strenuous
Terrain	Footpaths and tracks
Exposure	None
Highest point	1,903 metres

An interesting and varied walk to the peak of Cueva Valiente and along the Cuerda de la Carrasqueta ridge, in an area sprinkled with fortifications from the Spanish Civil War.

The walk starts next to the Camping Valle Enmedio campsite *(1)*. You can reach it from Alto del Leon, although the road is rough in places. The best, albeit longer, approach is from the village of Peguerinos as the road is better. Leave Peguerinos on Calle Real, a surfaced road heading east. Follow signs to Camping Valle de Enmedio. Turn left into the road leading to the campsite, marked with a wooden sign, and immediately before entering the campsite car park turn right into a small layby.

- Walk up the wide path heading north through the trees. You soon pass through a red gate and will walk parallel to a stream, which is on your left. Ignore paths on tangents to the left and right. The main path enters and runs along the bottom of the shallow valley of Valle de Enmedio, the sides of which you can see through the trees.

- After about 2 km, you'll see a sign to Cueva Valiente pointing up a now rocky path that ascends through the trees. Follow that path and you will soon come to a dilapidated, roofless building next to the path. Swing left here *(2)* to find the path behind the building, ascending the west flank of the valley.

- When you reach the col after about 500 metres, continue following the clear path heading straight ahead on the right-hand side of the col. This will soon bend right (north-east). Continue on that path, ignoring tangents and crossing any small clearings, and after about 1 km you will come to a fork *(3)* with three possibilities. Take the middle option, which looks like it will climb to the nearest small rocky outcrop to your right. It actually skirts around to the left of it and continues around towards the higher peak of Cueva Valiente, which you can see to the north. After 500 or so metres you arrive at a track that rises from your left.

- *If you want to visit some fortifications from the Spanish civil war, descend that track left. After 1 km you will encounter a sharp right-hand bend. Instead of taking the bend, head down a path to the left on the end of the bend. It will lead you down to a series of stone look-out points and fortifications. Return back up the hill to resume the walk.*

- Cueva Valiente *(4)* is the peak that you have before you, so head up the track (which you will see used to be surfaced) as it winds a short way up to the top, offering views of the eastern end of the Guadarrama range.

- Just to the right of the peak, between a refuge and a cluster of rocks, head down the path in a north-easterly direction. This path is initially steep and deeply grooved but the further you descend it turns to loose rock. Continue on that clear path all the way down to the valley floor, ignoring any tangents to the left and right.

- When it reaches the valley floor and levels out, follow the path as it swings sharp left. About 100 metres afterwards, a stream crosses the path (in summer it may be dry). Find a way over the stream to continue on the path straight ahead, which suddenly turns into a large track.

- After about 100 metres on the track, swing left onto a path through the trees *(5)*. You will shortly come to a stream and wooden bridge (and a gate to the left). Ignore those and swing right. You will start seeing posts with white/yellow markings. As you climb, you will cross the stream (or dry riverbed) on another small wooden bridge.

- A little further still and you will come to a sign with arrows pointing left and back from where you've just come from, with the words 'Senda Peña del Aguila'. Follow the arrow pointing left.

- You will arrive at a turnstile in a fence. However, before passing through the turnstile, take note of a rocky path heading up into the woods to the right, as you will be returning to it. Pass through the turnstile and visit the Mirador de la Peña del Aguila viewpoint and information board *(6)* on the left.

- Return through the turnstile and go left up the rocky path that you saw before. After 200 metres or so of climbing, you will arrive at a sharp bend in a track; ignore it and continue up the rocky path to your left. After a further 800 metres of ascent, you will arrive at a gravel road.

- Turn left up the road and you will soon arrive at the Collado de la Mina (the Col of the Mine), with a cattle grid. To the left of the cattle grid, follow the white/red painted stripes of the GR10 up to the top of Cabeza Lijar *(7)* – the peak directly in front of you – the summit of which contains a civil war bunker (now a refuge).

- After enjoying the views from the peak, return to Collado de la Mina, cross the road and follow the white/red GR10 markings in a south-westerly direction, keeping the fence to your left. At a fork keep right, and after 1.5 km you will arrive at the roofless building of Refugio La Salamanca. Continue past the ruin following the GR10, with a fence on your left, as it descends, passing through a gate. The path winds its way along the ridge of undulating peaks that you can see heading behind the huge cross of Valle de los Caidos (Valley of the Fallen), although you will not be going as far as the cross. The path skirts to the left of the rocky peak of Risco de Polanco and you will be accompanied by a wire fence, which is now on your right. This area is littered with the remains of civil war fortifications, turrets, living quarters, especially on the other side of the fence. After a while, you will pass through another gate.

- As you descend beyond Risco de Polanco, and still on the GR10, the path crosses a large clearing. Before re-entering the trees on the far side, you will see a path to your left (east) leading to a gate; ignore that. Instead, follow a sketchy path *(8)* to the right (west), which soon becomes more evident.

- This path meanders through the trees and you will eventually arrive at a dirt road. Turn right here and after 600 metres, swing left onto a path *(9)*. This path runs through the trees for 1 km or so and ultimately reaches a gravel road (although to reach it you have to cross a stream; there's an easy crossing approximately 30 metres to the left of the path). Once you are on the road turn left and follow it for 500 metres until you reach Camping Valle Enmedio.

CUEVA VALIENTE

APPROXIMATE GPS WAYPOINTS (UTM)

1	Valle Enmedio campsite	398403 4501350
2	Turn left at building	399016 4503337
3	Fork to Cueva Valiente	398979 4504218
4	Cueva Valiente	399212 4505000
5	Turn left off dirt track	400738 4505313
6	Mirador de la Peña del Aguila	400986 4505398
7	Cabeza Lijar	401947 4504949
8	Turn right onto sketchy path	401168 4501588
9	Turn left off dirt track	399867 4501119

Phil on the descent from Cueva Valiente - **WALK 4**

WALK NO. 5

WALK NO. 5 - CERRO DE SALAMANCA FROM ALTO DEL LEON

WALK NO. 5

CERRO DE SALAMANCA FROM ALTO DEL LEON

Distance	11.5 km
Ascent	500 metres
Overall grade	Easy
Terrain	Good footpaths and dirt roads
Exposure	None
Highest point	1,820 metres

A walk in and around the GR10 path on the broad ridge forming the border between the provinces of Madrid and Segovia. Although it is relatively easy, it reaches three hill tops and has great views and lots of points of interest.

This walk overlaps parts of Walk 4, but this walk is considerably easier and the circuit begins from the east, approaching the summits through different terrain.

- The walk starts and ends at Alto del León, also known as the Puerto de Guadarrama, at the top of the pass on the NVI highway *(1)*. You can find it by driving from the town of Guadarrama on the old road towards Segovia (not the A6 autovia). Driving north from Guadarrama, at the very top of the hill, there is a central island in the road. Turn left immediately beyond it. There is a bar/restaurant on the left side of the road with a minor road alongside it. Park here.

- Walk along the minor road going south-south-west. You will pass some ugly radio antennae but soon leave them behind. The road becomes a broad dirt track. At a cattle grid, go through the gate *(2)* and leave the main track, taking a path going uphill to the right. Red and white paint on a tree by the gate identifies this as the GR10. Do not go sharp right at the gate. Instead follow a path at a tangent, going gradually uphill south-west towards the top of a ridge, passing through Scots pine woods and with a barbed wire fence to the right. The path may be indistinct at times but as long as you do not cross the fence you will reach your destination.

- You will see signs saying 'Cabeza Lijar'. This does not mean that you have reached the said hilltop, but that you are on the way towards it. Keep looking for occasional white and red paint (possibly along with other colours).

- At the top of the hill (Cerro de la Gamonosa) there is a clearing. By the fence there is another Cabeza Lijar sign, and another one points to the left to 'Bunker', which is a relic of the Spanish Civil War (this was the frontier as the nationalists fought to take Madrid). The bunker *(3)* can be found some 50 metres from the main path, below some metal fencing. A ladder descends to the door.

- Return to the path, turn left and continue on the path to the south. Go downhill to a viewpoint with an information board. The path swings a little to the right and then continues with the fence still on the right. Your next target for this walk, Cabeza Lijar, is the hill you can see ahead. The fence eventually gives way to become a wall, which is still to your right.

- Continue downhill until, at an open green area, you reach the track you left earlier. Keep going in the same direction and a few metres farther on find a large gate *(4)* on the right, with paint marks showing that this remains the GR10. Go through the gate and turn left to follow the path uphill. There is now a wall to your left. Keep it there as you ascend, until after approximately 900 metres' distance, the path goes left to a gate in the wall. Go through the gate (fasten it as you leave) and keep going uphill until you reach the interesting summit of Cabeza Lijar, where you will find an old trig point, an information board (of no great interest) and the main attraction, which is another civil war bunker *(5)*. The roof of the bunker makes a viewpoint, and to one side there is another information board with a panorama naming the adjacent hills; a fine view.

- From the summit, continue down the far side of the hill. Ignore a green and white cross. It does not relate to this walk. There are rough concrete steps at first, and then the path continues downhill. It is eroded in places and people have taken short cuts. You can follow any of these. You will still occasionally see the white and red paint marks for reassurance.

- Soon you will reach a road once more (the same one you were on earlier) at Collado de la Mina. At the time of writing, the dirt track ends here and it becomes a well surfaced road. There is a large information board and map on the right, but the map covers a wide area and will not help you much.

- On reaching the road, go straight across and then uphill, with a wall to your left. At a fork, take the lower path to the right *(6)*, still marked occasionally with red and white. You will soon reach the ruined mountain refuge Refugio Salamanca *(7)*. This is the turning point for this walk.

- Go round to the far side of the building and turn left to reach the top of the hill, Cerro Salamanca. There are some boundary posts marking the top of the ridge. Crossing a few boulders you can walk more or less along the top of the ridge. Keep a fence to your right. You may need to slide down some boulders to reach easier ground, but basically you should follow the line of the ridge and descend gradually to reach the point where the outward path forked (6). From there, return to the broad track at Collado de la Mina, and turn right to follow the track all the way back to Alto del Leon.

- On the way, watch out for (i) where a small cabin stands in a meadow on the right; the track doubles back to the right. As you leave this bend, take a short cut downhill on stony ground to meet the track once more, and turn left along it; (ii) a little farther on, at a fork, keep left and stay on the higher track.
- You will eventually arrive at the gate near the start of the walk, just beyond which are the transmitters and then the main NVI road.

APPROXIMATE GPS WAYPOINTS (UTM)

1	Start	403699 4507222
2	Gate	403515 4506352
3	First bunker	403317 4505597
4	Big gate	402977 4505367
5	Cabeza Lijar	401952 4504951
6	Fork	401315 4504415
7	Refugio Salamanca	400930 4503946

WALK NO. 6

WALK NO. 6 - LA PEÑOTA

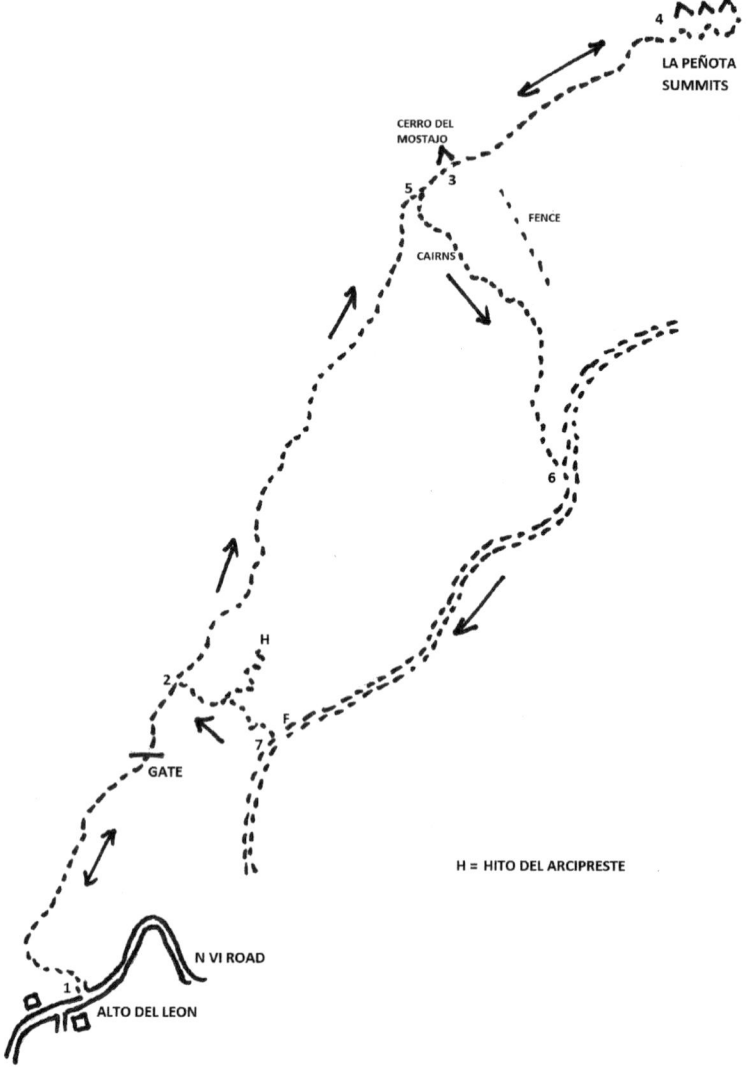

WALK NO. 6

LA PEÑOTA

Distance	17 km
Ascent	1,010 metres
Overall grade	Strenuous
Terrain	Mainly good footpaths, then a deteriorated path and a dirt road
Exposure	Minimal, and only at the summit
Highest point	1,936 metres

A walk on the eastern side of the NVI highway, along the broad ridge forming the border between the provinces of Madrid and Segovia. The route follows the GR10 to the summit of La Peñota, and then descends an old and little-used path marked with cairns. On the return leg the route visits the Peña del Arcipreste de Hita (see notes below).

- The walk starts and ends at Alto del León, also known as the Puerto de Guadarrama, on the NVI road at the very top of the pass. Find it by driving from the town of Guadarrama on the old road towards Segovia (not the A6 autovia). Driving north from Guadarrama, you can park on the right-hand side of the road at the very top of the hill. There is a signpost to the right-hand side of the road where a dirt track goes uphill and away from the road. Start here.

- Take the track by the signpost *(1)*, heading north-north-east. Within a few metres you will be unaware of the traffic you have left behind. The route follows the long-distance GR10 as far as the summit, so you can find your way by following its red and white paint marks. The path goes through sparse woodland, past some ruined buildings (civil war relics) and then descends somewhat, still going north-east. You will go gradually up and down a few times. About 1.25 kilometres from the start, keep straight ahead through a gate, and stay on the GR10. After a further 0.5 kilometres you will arrive at a junction. I call this the 'Arcipreste junction' *(2)*. Do not turn right, keep straight on.

- The path now starts a more continual ascent, crossing over a minor top (Peña el Cuervo) at 1,674 metres altitude, and then another (Peña Matalafuente) at 1,705 metres. Continue on the broad ridge. A broad track goes off to the left, but stay on the ridge path. You will cross another minor top (Cerro del Mostajo) *(3)* at 1,718 metres, and keeping straight on you will soon reach the rocky peak of La Peñota *(4)*. It has more than one summit, and the granite outcrops provide scrambling opportunities as well as good views. Take great care when scrambling, especially as the granite provides few handholds. The path skirts the rocks on their right-hand side. The summit post is on the second top. There is a poorly-marked route up it from its left side.

- From the summit, the alternatives depend on your transport facilities. If you are not dependent on returning to your vehicle at the start, you could continue on the ridge past La Peñota and take a footpath down to the right from the next col, to descend to Cercedilla. But the route described here takes you back to Alto del Leon, where you began the walk, by a somewhat different route.

- Return from La Peñota initially by the way you came, along the GR10, but less than 100 metres from the top of Cerro del Mostajo, cross the wall to the left *(5)* and look for cairns marking a route down to a dirt road some 320 metres below. This route is marked as a path on some maps, and indeed the cairns show the way, but they are not easy to follow. The path seems to have fallen into disuse, which is a shame because it makes a good route.

- Anyway, at GPS 405855 4510754 cross the wall to the south side and look for the cairns. As you start to descend you will encounter a wire fence. Do not cross the fence. Keep it on your left side and continue to descend diagonally across the slope of the hill. In general terms, the cairns follow the line of the fence. This part of the route is somewhat adventurous. If you lose the line of the cairns you will need to continue down the hill across rough terrain to reach the broad dirt track below and then turn right along it *(6)*.

- This is now easy walking. After about 2.5 kilometres on this track you should see a *fuente* on the right, and on a sharp left-hand bend *(7)* a narrow path ascends through woods, going north at first then north-west. It will take you back to the GR10, but before you reach it, look on the right for another path which goes uphill towards some elevated rocks, forming the Peña del Arcipreste de Hita *(8)*. There is an inscription on the rocky face. (See the note below.)

- From the Peña, return to the path you had been ascending from the dirt road below, and follow it uphill to a gate and the 'Arcipreste junction' *(2)*, where you should turn left to return to the start.

APPROXIMATE GPS WAYPOINTS (UTM)

1	Start and finish	403699 4507222
2	'Arcipreste junction'	404522 4508630
3	Cerro del Mostajo	405915 4510784
4	First summit	407078 4511364
5	Top of hill and start of cairned path down	405855 4510754

WALK NO. 6

6	Turn right on dirt road	406461 4509775
7	Path up	404952 4508370
8	Peña del Arcipreste de Hita	404651 4508562

NOTES: PEÑA DEL ARCIPRESTE DE HITA

An 'arcipreste' is a high priest. Juan Ruiz, a 13th/14th century poet, was also a priest in the village of Hita in the province of Guadalajara. In 1930, the Spanish Royal Academy had an inscription made on these rocks in his honour.

Phil on La Penota - **WALK 6**

LA MUJER MUERTA FROM ORTIGOSA DEL MONTE (SEGOVIA)

WALK NO. 7 - LA MUJER MUERTA FROM THE NORTH SIDE

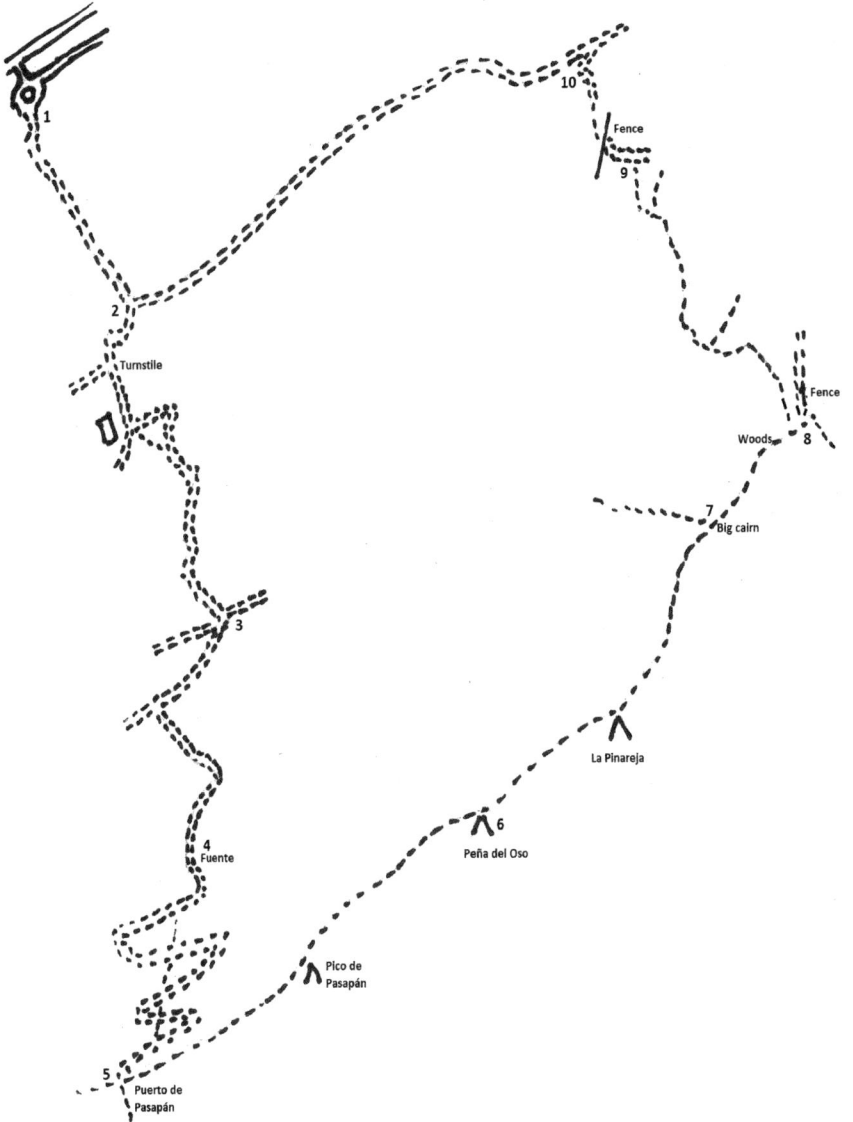

WALK NO. 7

LA MUJER MUERTA FROM ORTIGOSA DEL MONTE (SEGOVIA)

Distance	25 km
Ascent	1,275 metres
Overall grade	Very strenuous
Terrain	Good tracks and footpaths, and some boulders
Exposure	None
Highest point	2,198 metres

A strenuous traverse of a broad ridge. Underfoot the going is mainly easy, although there are one or two short boulder fields to be crossed. The circuit is classed as very strenuous due to the overall distance and ascent rather than any technical difficulty.

- There are three tops along the ridge, Pico de Pasapan (1,988 metres), Peña del Oso (2,197 metres) and La Pinareja (2,198 metres). The whole ridge is known as La Mujer Muerta – the Dead Woman – because local sources say that from the north it resembles a prostrate lady. I have to admit that I have not been able to discern this myself. It is a great walk all the same.

- The walk begins close to a main road near the village of Ortigosa del Monte. Travelling towards Segovia on the N603, shortly after kilometre 81, turn right into a minor road. In case of doubt, look for a round building on the right with a domed roof and park near it. This road runs parallel to the main road. There is a roundabout where a dirt track goes to the south-east. Walk up the dirt track *(1)*. You will see an information board showing two routes, one to the top of Pico del Oso and back, and the other a shorter route along the

- northern slopes ('Laderas') of the hills. Our route is a circular one, and is more demanding than the routes on the signpost.

- Walk along the dirt road for about 1.5 kilometres, and at a junction take the right fork *(2)*, where a sign shows the start of the routes. The track, part of the GR88, zig-zags up and comes to a gate with a turnstile. Go through it and continue. You will see what seems to be a deserted ranch, and a signpost shows the way to the Laderas de Mujer Muerta. Turn left here, then take a path up to the right to short cut the bends. When you reach the track again, turn right. At a four-way junction *(3)* go up to the right, on the most uphill of the tracks, following the sign to Puerto de Pasapan. At a crossroads with a big post, at 1,524 metres altitude, turn left.

- Stay on the main track. You will soon pass a *fuente (4)*, refreshing on a warm day. You should see a yellow and white marker, and the terrain opens out above a green valley. You will reach a gate, but just before it you have a choice. The more direct and steeper route follows a footpath to the left, up the valley bottom. The broader track takes wider zigzags to arrive at the same place. If you follow the track you will see another sign for Puerto de Pasapan, and then go through a turnstile gate near a viewpoint (Mirador de Milanillos) with a wooden fence. Go sharply to the right.

- Whether you take the broad track or the footpath, you will soon reach the pass at Puerto de Pasapán *(5)*. Turn left here to follow the top of the ridge to the north-east. There is hardly any need for directions here. Just follow the high ground. You will cross all three summits, Pico Pasapán, Peña del Oso *(6)* and La Pinareja. The latter is marginally the highest.

- Pico del Oso means the 'Peak of the Bear'. On the trig point there are statues of two small bears. There is a large cairn on the summit of La Pinareja. There are some boulders to be crossed between these two peaks. The route is marked with cairns, but if in doubt stay high and keep going north-east.

- Continue over the all three summits, and then keep straight ahead, now going north-north-east and downhill. You may see some marker posts and/or cairns going away to your left, but ignore them. They lead to a very difficult scree slope. Instead, stay on the highest ground as you descend. From a large cairn *(7)*, keep going north-east towards a wooded area below. There is an intermittent path down here, but you will be crossing rocks and boulders at times. Keep going past more cairns and into the woods. Again the path is intermittent, but if you keep going in the same direction and stay on high ground you will eventually arrive at a clearing, the col of the Rio Peces *(8)*.

- At the meadow on the col, look for a fenced area and a boundary post on the left. Turn left immediately before the fence, but do not follow the broad track going down to the north. Instead, go further left and look for a rock amongst the trees marking the start of a footpath going to the north of west. This very nice path descends gradually through Scots pine woods. Ignore a minor path going down to the right, and just beyond it you will cross the bottom end of a massive scree slope. Stay on the path, which becomes a lovely grassy track with a stream valley below on the right. Soon the path swings left. Ignore another minor path down to the right. The path descends somewhat more steeply. You will reach a broader track. Turn left along it *(9)* then go through a turnstile or a gate through a fence. Take the path which goes down from the gate and swings to the right. This brings you down to some green fields with holm oak trees dotted around and you should soon have a wall to your right.

- The path becomes a broader track with grass down the middle. It soon bends to the right to join a more important dirt road. Turn left along the major dirt road *(10)*, which is marked with red markers for the GR88. Continue along this track for about 3.5 easy kilometres until you reach the junction of tracks *(2)* 1.5 kilometres from where the walk began. Turn right here and walk back down the track to the start.

APPROXIMATE GPS WAYPOINTS (UTM)

1	Start and finish	403680 4521816
2	Keep right	404424 4520572
3	Four-way junction	405094 4518676
4	Fuente	404993 4517122
5	Puerto de Pasapán	404537 4516011
6	Peña del Oso	406861 4517595
7	Cairn (straight on)	408317 4519473
8	Collado de Rio Peces	408977 4520115
9	Go left to gate/turnstile	407869 4521238
10	Dirt road back to first junction	406449 4522133

WALK NO. 8

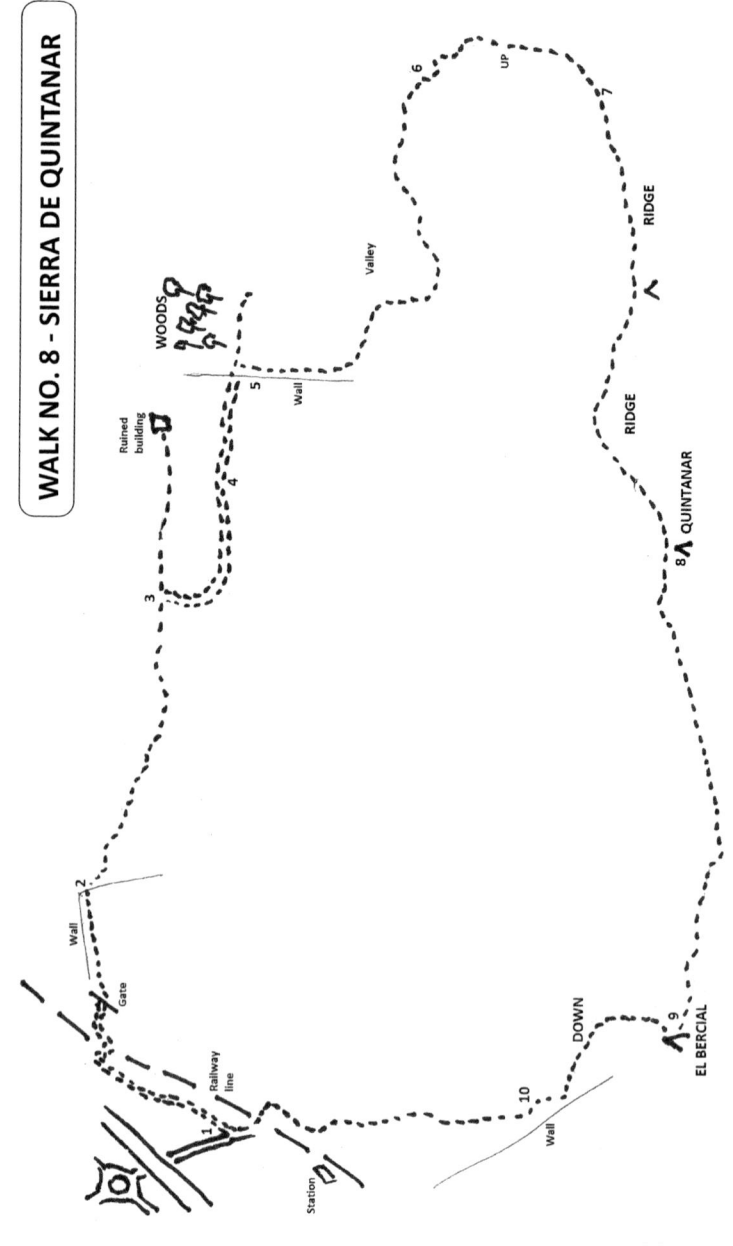

WALK NO. 8

SIERRA DE QUINTANAR

Distance	16 km
Ascent	980 metres
Overall grade	Moderate
Terrain	Footpaths, good tracks and some off-piste walking on grass
Exposure	None
Highest point	2,004 metres

An ascent to the continuation of the ridge, going west from the sierra of La Mujer Muerta. The most prominent summit on the ridge, Quintanar (also sometimes known as Cerro Camochin), is not in fact the highest point, which is where we first reach the crest of the ridge at Peñas de la Majada.

- The walk starts and ends at the Urbanizacion Canalejos, close to the town of Otero de Herreros. To find it, driving from the town of Guadarrama, take the NVI then the N603, go past San Rafael and continue as far as a roundabout where a left turn goes to Otero de Herreros. Instead of turning left to the town, turn right at the roundabout and cross over the motorway. Go straight on for about 400 metres and park at a junction of tracks on the left *(1)*.

- Walk along the track going north-east for about 700 metres then turn right to cross the railway line. You will reach a green gate, which may be padlocked but there are steps to its right. Go over the steps, turn left and follow a wall.

- After 600 metres, cross the wall where it swings to the right *(2)*, then follow the wall as a vague path leads up to reach an old water building. Then join a broader track and go up it, heading generally south-east. After about 600 metres, follow a track going to the right *(3)*, at first to the south then swinging back to the south-east. Waypoint *(4)* below will help you to confirm that you are on the right track. Stay on the track, which reaches a wall by some woods. Cross the wall and turn right *(5)*, to walk across open country with the wall to your right. Stay near the wall for about 1 kilometre, and then follow the contour across the head of a valley, swinging to the left (east).

- There are several tracks in this area, which can be confusing. Just continue going just north of east for a further 700 metres to waypoint *(6)*, where you can swing to the south-east and begin a steady ascent towards the ridge above. Use your intuition to follow the nose of a hill leading up to the ridge to the south, and after about 1.3 kilometres, including some zigzagging about, you should reach the ridge at about 2,004 metres altitude *(7)*. This is the highest point on the Quintanar sierra. Turn right (west) to follow the ridge as it crosses various minor tops, each of them above 1,900 metres. These are the Peñas de la Majadas. The terrain is moorland, and you should just keep to the high ground. There is a wall along it at times.

- After 2.5 kilometres along the ridge, you will reach the trig point at the official summit of Quintanar at 1,932 metres, from where the descent begins *(8)*. Before commencing the descent you may like to visit a memorial cross, which stands a few metres to the west. From the summit, follow a steep path downhill to the west alongside a wall with a rusty iron fence. The descent seems never ending! But it levels out and 2.5 kilometres from the top it reaches a minor, rocky summit, El Bercial *(9)*, with some broken-down fencing. You can visit the summit and then descend to its eastern side, from where you should go downhill to the north-north-west. There is no clear path now, and most of the remaining descent is across open country. Go through a wall and then keep to the right of the next wall going downhill. Waypoint *(10)* is alongside the wall, which you can follow down towards the railway line. Look ahead for the station and go straight towards it. Opposite the station, turn right to follow the railway and you can cross the line on a dirt track, which leads back to the start.

APPROXIMATE GPS WAYPOINTS (UTM)

1	Start and finish	398504 4517718
2	Cross the wall	399539 4518451
3	Track to the south	400268 4518225
4	On the track	401317 4518087
5	Wall by the woods	401868 4517891
6	Ascend to the south-east	402765 4517075
7	Ridge top	403255 4516245
8	Last main summit (Quintanar)	401197 4515748
9	El Bercial	398962 4515695
10	Wall	398634 4516353

WALK NO. 9

WALK NO. 9 - CERRO DEL AGUILA AND PEÑA BERCIAL

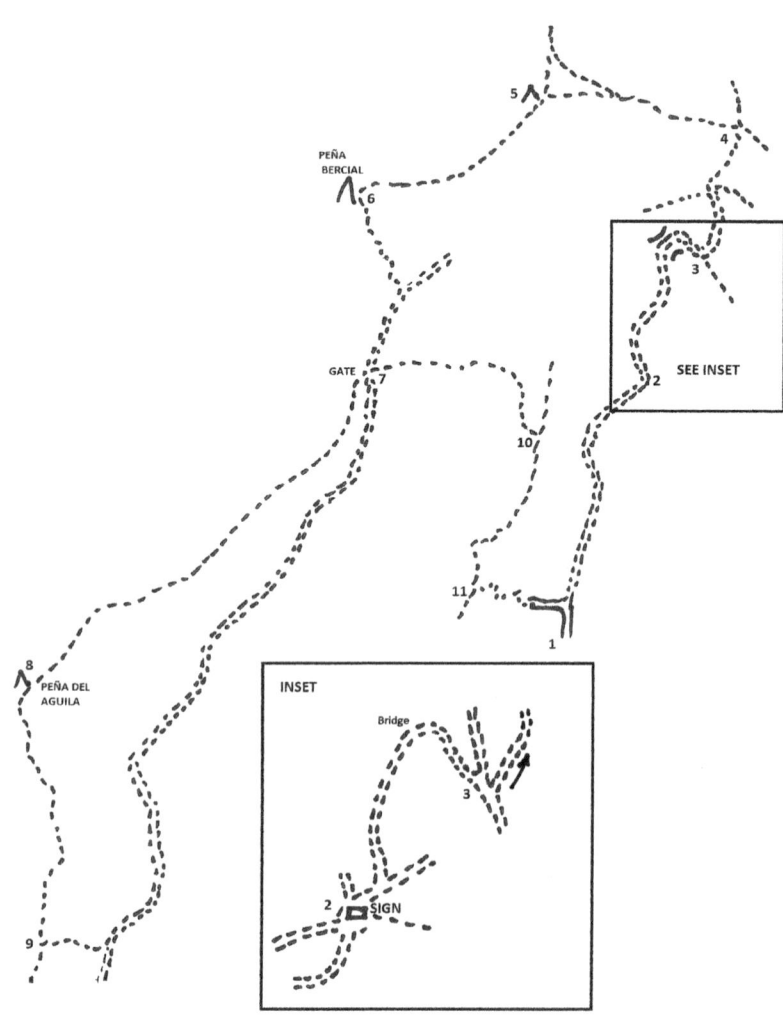

WALK NO. 9

CERRO DEL AGUILA AND PEÑA BERCIAL

Distance	19 km
Ascent	995 metres
Overall grade	Moderate
Terrain	Mainly good footpaths, some broad dirt tracks and a little off-piste navigation
Exposure	None
Highest point	2,023 metres

A walk from the popular valley of Las Dehesas to three summits on the long-distance GR10. This is a very popular area with Madrileños, so expect to see other walkers.

A section of this walk is off-piste, and requires some navigation. It could be difficult in mist.

- The walk starts and ends at the car park of Las Dehesas, near Cercedilla. From the centre of the town, drive west towards the railway station. As the road swing sharply to the left just before the station, turn sharp right where Las Dehesas is signposted. You will soon enter a one-way system. Keep right at any forks in the tarmac road (don't turn off onto minor tracks). About 3.5 kilometres from the town you will reach an area where several car parks are signposted with letters A, B, C, etcetera. Park in any of these.

- There are picnic tables and a *fuente* in the woods here, and opposite car park C there is a bar, which is open at peak times.

- From Car Park C *(1)*, walk up the road to the north for 400 metres. At a 90-degree left-hand bend in the road, go straight ahead past a barrier on a broad dirt road. You are now walking in the valley of Fuenfria, and your first aim will be to reach the Puerto de Fuenfria (Fuenfria Pass), which is about 3 kilometres to the north-east.

- Go past some rusty metal signs showing the route of an old Roman road (a route to Segovia from Madrid. It became abandoned when the easier route via Puerto de Navacerrada was opened). Cross a bridge signposted: Calzada Romana (Roman road). Keep straight on until you come to a clearing *(2)* where an engraved wooden sign vaguely shows some of the routes in the area. Several different tracks leave this point. Take the track uphill just slightly to the right, but after only a few metres there is a metal sign on the left for the Roman road. Take this path uphill. The signs indicate the way to Fuenfria.

- The path becomes stony (almost paved) and there are white paint marks on the trees. Ignore a path going slightly downhill to the right and stay on this track, which will swing to the east and cross a bridge. After another 300 metres at a junction, turn left *(3)*. There are two tracks going left here. Ignore the sharpest left turn. Follow the right-hand one directly up to the Puerto de Fuenfria *(4)*, a broad meadow on the provincial border between Madrid and Segovia. There are some boundary posts and signposts.

- There are several routes from here, but for this walk turn left (west) and uphill, to ascend the slopes of Cerro Minguete. To avoid doubt, from the Puerto do not take a good track to the south-west. Instead, take a footpath which goes directly up the hill very slightly north of west. The path goes through heather and other undergrowth. It separates at times but normally these branches of the path rejoin each other. The correct route keeps to the high ground all the way.

- Soon you will reach the summit of Cerro Minguete (2,023 metres altitude) *(5)*, and there are great views in all directions. At the summit turn left. Walk along the top of the broad ridge to the south-west and simply keep to the highest ground for a little over a kilometre of easy walking. The route veers to the west and ascends slightly to reach the top of Peña Bercial *(6)* (2,002 metres). The summit is a rocky area and it is not entirely obvious which bit is the official summit. If you are using GPS you can scramble up the rocks to get yourself to the 2,000 metre mark.

- From Peña Bercial the route is somewhat difficult to follow. There is no obvious path. Looking to the south from the summit, you should see a dirt road well below. Your next targets are that dirt road and the next hill, Peña del Aguila. From the top of Pena Bercial there are cairns marking the way down. This is a relatively difficult off-piste section of the walk. The cairns are difficult to follow, but you should find one at GPS 408954 4515649, where you go slightly to the right and then try to find other cairns which lead you to the dirt road GPS 409041 4515284. Turn right along the dirt road to reach a gate where a path goes down to the left *(7)*. This is the Marichiva col. You will return here later in the walk, so this downhill path is a short-cut option. For the full walk, go through the gate on the right and take the path uphill to the right-hand side of the wall, which you can follow to the summit of Peña del Aguila (the Hill of the Eagle) *(8)* at 2,001 metres.

- Continue over the top of the hill going south and follow the highest ground, until at 1.3 kilometres from the top of Aguila you reach a lower col where a path goes through the wall to the left *(9)*. This path will lead you down to a dirt road. Turn left along it, and after about 3.5 kilometres you will be back at the Marichiva col *(7)*. Turn right here and descend on a stony path.

Follow the path downhill through trees. After roughly 1 kilometre the path swings left, and then after a further 300 metres, another path comes in from the left *(10)*. Turn right here and follow this path down. You will soon reach an open area with a stream *(11)*. Turn left here and continue on a path downhill, following the stream, to reach a road. Go straight across it and it will bring you to the top end of the car park areas from where you began the walk.

APPROXIMATE GPS WAYPOINTS (UTM)

1	Start	409760 4513526
2	Clearing	410167 4514961
3	Turn left	410488 4515542
4	Puerto de Fuenfria	410582 4516240
5	Cerro Minguete	409726 4516429
6	Pena Bercial	408969 4515895
7	Marichiva	408928 4514937
8	Pena del Aguila	407455 4513283
9	Path	407621 4512072
10	Path junction	409661 4514317
11	Turn left	407621 4512072

MONTON DE TRIGO

WALK NO. 10 - MONTON DE TRIGO

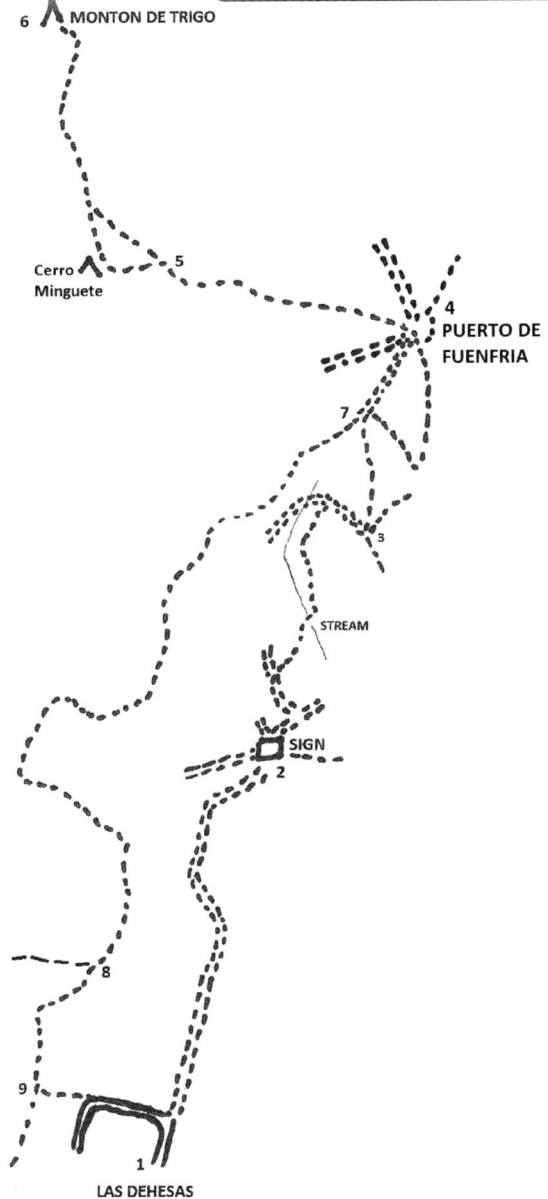

WALK NO. 10

MONTON DE TRIGO

Distance	12 km
Ascent	803 metres
Overall grade	Easy
Terrain	Good tracks and footpaths
Exposure	None
Highest point	2,149 metres

A walk from the popular valley of Las Dehesas to the Puerto de Fuenfria and then to a relatively easy but dominant peak. The name of the mountain, Monton de Trigo, means Mountain of Wheat, evidently due to its conical shape when seen from the south.

Parts of this walk are similar to Walk 9. The outward part of the route covers the same area, but uses different paths where possible. The final 350 metres are identical to the other walk. The two walks can be combined to make for a longer and more strenuous route.

- The walk starts and ends at Car Park C at Las Dehesas *(1)*.

- Walk up the road past the car parking areas, and as the tarmac road swings 90 degrees left, walk straight ahead past a barrier on a broad track. Go past some rusty metal signs showing the route of the old Roman road. Cross a bridge signposted: Calzada Romana (Roman road). Keep straight on until you come to a clearing where an engraved wooden sign vaguely shows some of the routes in the area *(2)*.

- There are lots of paths going off from here. Take the track just slightly to the right but after only a few metres there is a metal sign on the left for the Roman road. Take this path uphill. The signs indicate the way to Fuenfria.

MONTON DE TRIGO

- The path becomes stony (almost paved) and there are white paint marks on the trees, but after a very short distance look for a path going slightly downhill to the right, with a green paint mark on a tree. Take this path. It passes another rusty iron signpost.

- There is a little wooden bridge to the right, but ignore it and keep to the left side of the stream. You will soon cross the stream and there are more Calzada Romana signs. Now follow the path uphill with the stream on your left and green marks on the trees. At a little junction where a path goes up to the right, keep straight ahead past another metal roman road sign. Keep the stream to your left. The path almost disappears, but continue and you will reach a large bridge where a track crosses the stream. Go up to the bridge and turn right along the track. It is now a stony track again with white markers on the trees. At the next junction *(3)* a stony track goes up to the left, but a sharper turn to the left is marked with another metal marker. Take that lower and easier (at first) path.

- You will now be following green paint marks. (Don't ask me to explain all this paint!)

- At the next junction swing right uphill. Good views open up behind. There are two paths going uphill here, and a signpost which is not very clear. Take the right-hand of these paths, the stony one.

- Soon you will cross a junction with another path (the Borbonica route) but go straight ahead by more rusty iron markers. At the next marker swing left, and continue uphill. You will then reach the pass *(4)* (Puerto de Fuenfria). There is a gate ahead, with a rocky barrier round a clearing on the right. A good track goes to the left, but ignore it and go uphill on a somewhat eroded path on the left (west) to ascend the slopes of Cerro Minguete.

- The path separates at times and rejoins itself. There are intermittent cairns. Just keep going straight uphill in so far as you can. After about 500 metres from leaving Puerto de Fuenfria, look for cairns taking you to the right *(5),* and staying below the summit. A path here takes you directly to the col immediately below Monton de Trigo, which stands above the col as a pyramid-shaped peak. Turn right at the col and follow a good path towards the mountain. As the path swings left look for minor paths going straight up the hill ahead. There is more than one path and there are cairns in various places. It doesn't really matter which one you are on. Just follow the cairns uphill, with bits of boulder scrambling, until you reach the summit of Monton de Trigo *(6).* The views are exceptional.

- Return by the way you came, as far as the Puerto de Fuenfria. Once you are back at the Puerto, do not take the broad track to the south-east. Look for the Roman Road, but instead of taking it descend a path to its right, down a short and loose section into a valley. You will see white and yellow paint markers and should be going just west of south. Stay on this path. Following the yellow and white all the way should lead you almost back to the start of the walk.

- At one point you will reach a junction of paths which you encountered on the ascent *(7).* The roman road goes down to the left, but take the path straight ahead. It is still marked yellow and white, and is in generally good condition. Cross a bridge over a stream, and later a second bridge with a little *fuente* on the right before it. Just keep going until you meet a track coming down from the right *(8)* which is marked with red paint. Do not ascend this, but keep left and follow the track downhill. On a tree you should see white and yellow paint and also a red mark.

- You will soon reach another junction just before a stream, where a tree in the middle of the path has white and yellow paint, but another tree beyond it and to the right has a red paint mark. Take a left turn by the white and yellow marker *(9)* and go downhill. At a barbed wire fence go through a gate and continue straight downhill. Reaching a track an old path goes ahead past some barriers, but you can take a right and a left to avoid them (they are there to reduce erosion, I think.) Join a tarmac road and turn left along it and downhill to reach the red and white barrier at the start of the walk.

APPROXIMATE GPS WAYPOINTS (UTM)

1	Start	409760 4513526
2	Clearing	410167 4514961
3	Sharp left	410488 4515542
4	Puerto de Fuenfria	410582 4516240
5	Keep right	410070 4516359
6	Monton de Trigo	409644 4517121
7	Junction – straight on	410422 4515949
8	Junction – straight on	409661 4514317
9	Turn left	409546 4513930

WALK NO. 11

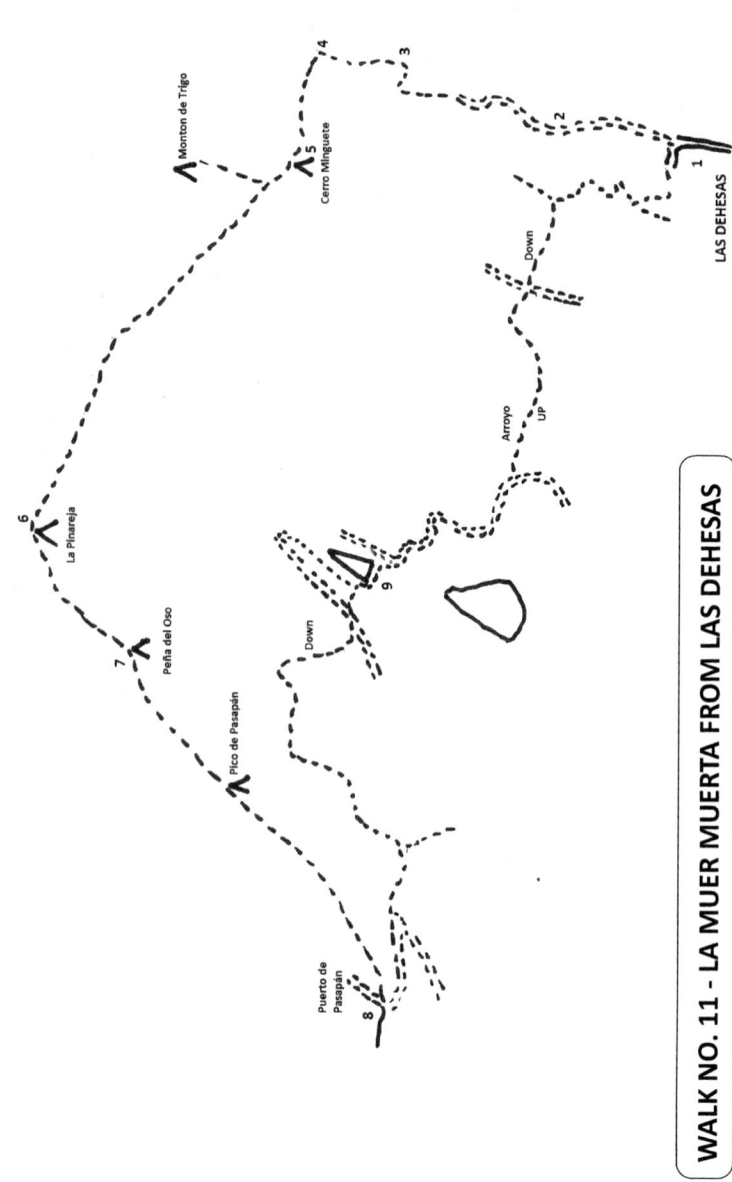

WALK NO.11

LA MUJER MUERTA FROM LAS DEHESAS (CERCEDILLA)

Distance	21 km
Ascent	1205 metres
Overall grade	Strenuous
Terrain	Good tracks and footpaths, and some boulders
Exposure	None
Highest point	2,198 metres

Walk 7 is a traverse of the Mujer Muerta ridge, starting and finishing on the northern, Segovia side of the sierra. This walk takes the more popular route from the Madrid side, along the same ridge but in the opposite direction.

The walk begins and ends at Las Dehesas, near Cercedilla. Parts of this walk coincide with Walks 9 and 10, which begin in the same place. All three walks explore the Fuenfria valley, where several different paths cover the same general area. This walk varies from Walk 9 by traversing the higher and more remote ridge.

- For this route, follow the instructions set out in Walk 9 as far as Cerro Minguete, waypoint *(5)*. From there follow these directions.

- At the summit of Cerro Minguete, turn right and follow a good path along the ridge top towards the pyramid peak of Monton de Trigo. You may go over that peak if you wish, but the walk is strenuous enough without that, so stay on the path which skirts the bottom of that hill, heading north-west. The path crosses the broad col Collado de Tirobarra, at just below the 2,000 metres altitude then ascends to the top of La Pinareja, 2,194 metres *(6)*. Turn left along the broad ridge. This is the beginning of La Mujer Muerta, and for about the next 5 kilometres you will be doing the reverse route of Walk 7.

- Keep to the high ground and continue across the summits of Pico del Oso *(7)* and Pico de Pasapán, before descending to the col at Puerto de Pasapán *(8)*. Here you should turn left and head into the valley to the east. From the pass there is a good dirt track. After about 700 metres the track swings back on itself sharp right, but do not follow it round the bend. Instead, go straight ahead on a minor path. After another 350 metres, ignore a track going down to the right and instead swing to the left, ascending slightly. The path continues to the north-east.

- About 2 kilometres along this path, it swings to the right and goes downhill to meet a broad forestry track *(9)*. Turn left along it for about 350 metres, then to save distance leave the track at a convenient point and descend to where the track goes alongside a reservoir. Walk across the dam *(10)* then ascend a path for a few metres to join a dirt track again. Go to the right along the track and stay on it for almost 2 kilometres until it crosses the Arroyo (stream) Las Tabladillas. Cross the bridge and then take a path to the left with the stream below on your left. This leads uphill to reach another major track at Collado de Marichiva *(11)*. From here the descent is the same as in Walk 9, but to save too much cross-referencing I repeat the directions here.

- Go straight across the broad track at Marichiva and descend on a stony path. Follow the path downhill through trees. After roughly 1 kilometre the path swings left, and then after a further 300 metres, another path comes in from the left. Turn right here and follow this path down. You will soon reach an open area with a stream. Turn left here and continue on a

LA MUJER MUERTA FROM LAS DEHESAS (CERCEDILLA)

path downhill, following the stream, to reach a road. Go straight across it and it will bring you to the top end of the car park areas from which you began the walk.

APPROXIMATE GPS WAYPOINTS (UTM)

1	Start and finish	409760 4513526
2	Clearing	410167 4514961
3	Turn left	410488 4515542
4	Puerto de Fuenfria	410582 4516240
5	Cerro Minguete	409726 4516429
6	La Pinareja	407712 4518260
7	Pico del Oso	406861 4517595
8	Puerto de Pasapán	404537 4516011
9	Forestry track	406771 4516258
10	Cross the dam	406786 4515159
11	Collado de Marichiva	408928 4514937

La Mujer Muerta - **WALK 11**

WALK NO. 12

WALK NO. 12 - MIRADOR LUIS ROSALES AND MAJALASNA

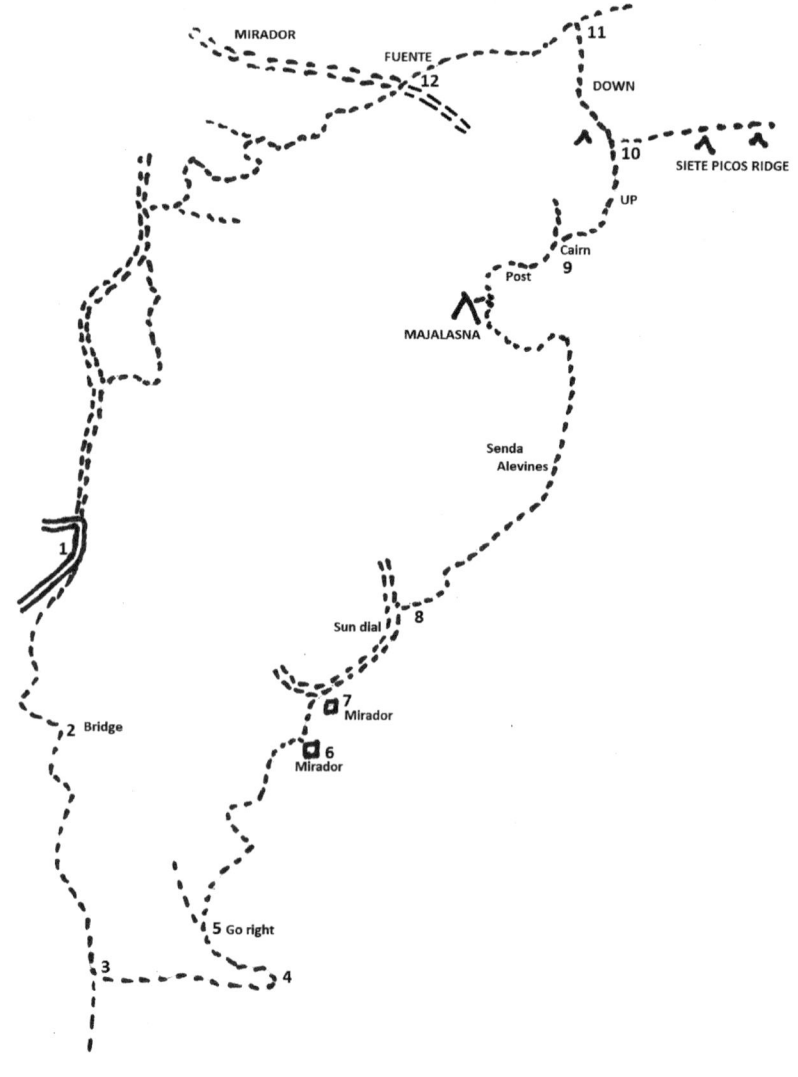

WALK NO. 12

MIRADOR LUIS ROSALES AND MAJALASNA

Distance	16 km
Ascent	850 metres
Overall grade	Moderate to strenuous
Terrain	Good footpaths
Exposure	None, unless you do the optional scrambles
Highest point	2,056 metres

A circuit from the recreation area at Las Dehesas, near Cercedilla. The route goes to Majalasna, the lowest of the Siete Picos (Seven Peaks) and then crosses the ridge of the higher six peaks. The return is via Collado Ventoso and the Fuenfria valley.

At Majalasna and at the higher ridge, there are opportunities for scrambling, which would be extra to these statistics. There is also an option to start and finish the walk in the village of Cercedilla. This adds 8 kilometres in total, making it a strenuous day.

- The walk begins at car park 'C' at Las Dehesas. To find it from the centre of Cercedilla, take the road to the west towards Guadarrama (the M622), and at a sharp left-hand bend just before the railway station, turn right where Las Dehesas is signposted. After about 2.5 kilometres, take the right fork. You will pass some buildings with car parks, but the main public car parks are marked with letters 'A', 'B', 'C' and so on. Car park C is on the left, opposite a bar/restaurant (which is open at busy times). If this car park is full, park elsewhere but these walk directions start at car park C.

- Leaving the car park *(1)* walk back down the road (south), but turn left quickly to cross a grassy area and descend to a gate in front of some buildings. At the gate, turn right on a path next to a fence. Look to your left and find a small bridge *(2)* crossing a stream. The path is shown by yellow paint marks on trees. Cross the bridge and turn right. Do not take the path next to the stream, but follow the higher path to its left. There are more yellow paint marks, marking a route which we will follow during much of this walk.

- Go through a gate. Shortly afterwards, at a junction take the left fork *(3)*. The path is soon going east, and as it enters a clearing, where a tree on the right has a yellow paint mark, the path swings sharply to the left. If you miss it and cross the clearing you will start going downhill. If so, go back and find the turn *(4)*. Follow this path, now heading north-west. Soon there is another slight problem. The main path appears to go straight ahead, but yellow marks show that our route goes uphill to the right *(5)*, at first over eroded ground.

- When the path levels out there is a low kind of wall on your right. Turn to the right here and it takes you to the Luis Rosales viewpoint *(6)*. (Rosales was a local poet). On leaving the viewpoint, take the path to the north, which leads you to a broad track, where there is a second viewpoint on your right, this one being the Mirador Vicente Alexander *(7)*. Turn right here and go along a broad track. Soon, as the track swings to the right, on your left you will find the strange sun-dial, El Reloj de la Cela (see notes below). Just beyond here is a green clearing with a signpost *(8)* to the right of the track. Three paths lead off to the right of the clearing. Take the one going north and then very soon north-east. It is called the Senda Alevines and is marked again with yellow paint; and now also with yellow and white marks. It goes uphill through pine woods. Eventually, as you leave the woods, the peak of Majalasna is directly in front of you.

- Keep going to the right-hand side of the pile of rocks which form the peak. The route goes to the right but it is possible to scramble to the top before you continue. It is easier with somebody to lend a hand. Take care of course.

- From the right-hand (eastern) side of the peak the path then goes up to the right through heather to a small ridge. There is a large cairn on top of a rock, and just beyond it another smaller cairn marks the start of a minor path to the right of the main one *(9)*. Take this minor path here, and also leave the yellow paint, and follow this path which is marked with cairns. It leads you to the top of the Siete Picos ridge, to the right-hand side of the first peak *(10)*. Continue across the top of the ridge and straight down the far side, going north. This will lead you down to Collado Ventoso, the Windy Col *(11)*.

- Collado Ventoso is a broad, green and fairly flat area. A number of paths and tracks leave it, so you need to find the right one. For this route, follow the Camino Schmid, which starts as a broad track going just south of west. To find the correct route, look for more yellow paint marks. The path leads you downhill steadily. At a junction take the right fork. Continue down to reach a broad dirt track by a *fuente* with a wooden bench *(12)*. The route continues straight down the other side of the track, but if you wish you can make side-trip to see the viewpoint Mirador de la Reina, which is about 350 metres along the dirt track to the right. From there you look down the whole of the Fuenfria valley, and on the right are the hills of Aguila, Penota, Abantos and in the distance las Machotas. But then return to the *fuente* and continue down the path.

- You will meet a track coming down from the right. This is the old Roman Road, but we are following the Camino Schmid. The two routes coincide for a short distance. So, turn left down the track. Soon an iron signpost shows where the Roman Road turns right, but go past it and follow the track round the next bend. As before, follow the yellow marks. You will reach a dirt road. Turn right, to cross a bridge over a stream. Once you have crossed the bridge, walk down the track then take a path to the left to follow the stream.

- You will soon reach some gate posts and metal signs. Here, turn off the main track going to the left, pass another iron marker post and now ignore the yellow marks and start to follow green markers. Go through a kind of metal gateway (which I don't think was built by the Romans!) and then turn left down a stony track to a bridge (the Puente del Descalzo). This track will take you back to the start of the walk.

APPROXIMATE GPS WAYPOINTS (UTM)

1	Start and finish	409760 4513526
2	Bridge	409843 4513077
3	Left fork	409925 4512109
4	Sharp left	410587 4512053
5	Keep right	410379 4512226
6	Mirador (viewpoint)	410797 4513018
7	Second mirador	410823 4513163
8	Signpost	411313 4513665
9	Cairn for path junction	411534 4514851
10	Top of ridge	411970 4515256
11	Collado Ventoso	411809 4515824
12	Fuente	411115 4515581

MIRADOR LUIS ROSALES AND MAJALASNA

NOTES: *Camilo Jose Cela was a Nobel prize-winning writer, who was an aficionado of these hills. The sun dial was created in his memory. It is interactive. You can stand within it and your shadow should show you the time.*

Majalasna - **WALK 12**

WALK NO. 13

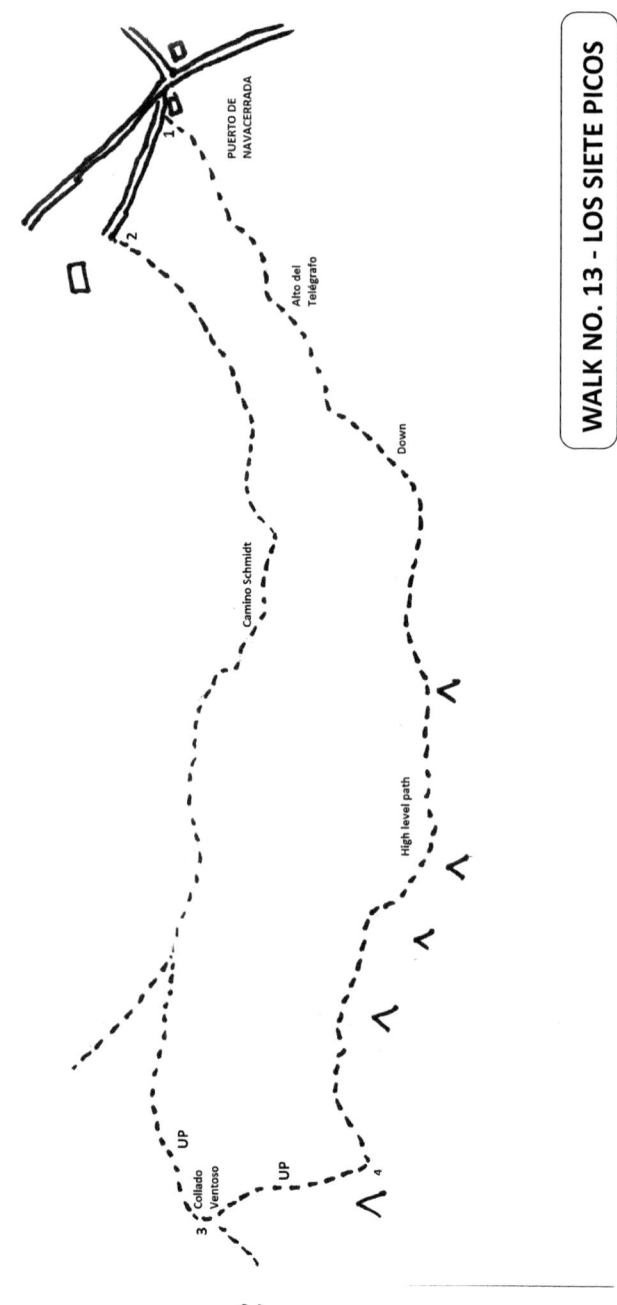

WALK NO. 13

LOS SIETE PICOS (THE SEVEN PEAKS)

Distance	11 km
Ascent	570 metres
Overall grade	Easy
Terrain	Good quality footpaths and optional scrambles
Exposure	None, other than on the scrambles
Highest point	2,138 metres

A popular circular walk along an easy trail through delightful Scots pine woods, then a traverse on good paths alongside a series of granite peaks, some of which can be reached by scramblers.

The 'Siete Picos' are a line of six granite outcrops along the top of a broad ridge, plus a seventh, lower peak called Majalasna (which is included in Walk 12). The Siete Picos ridge is very prominent from the towns to the south of the sierra de Guadarrama, and they are easily accessible from the Puerto de Navacerrada. The latter has large car parks and a train connection to the nearby town of Cercedilla.

- The walk begins at the Puerto de Navacerrada, on the M601, at the top of the hill on the border between the provinces of Madrid and Segovia. In winter this is a ski resort, and there is a large car park. It can also be reached by the mountain train from the town of Cercedilla. Timetables are on www.renfe.es.

- Start the walk at the crest of the hill on the main road *(1)*. At the crossroads take a tarmac lane leading north-west. There is a fenced-off ski slope above to your left. Follow the lane and you will soon see signs for the

'Camino Schmid'. After half a kilometre you will see a military building ahead, and the Camino Schmid trail goes into the Scots pine woods to the left. Follow this easy path *(2)*, which is well marked with paint on the trees, and although I hesitate to use the term, you can't really go wrong.

- The Scots pines provide shade in hot weather, but due to their high-level foliage they permit light to enter and there are views to the north. The forest makes for very nice walking. If you are here at the weekend you will find plenty of other walkers.

- The path crosses a ski piste. If there is still snow on the ground it can be slippery, so take care. Otherwise you have no decisions to make along here until after about 3 kilometres, when you will reach a fork in the path. Take the left fork, uphill.

- The route starts to ascend gradually, still in the pine woods, until after 400 metres distance and 60 metres' ascent, you will arrive at a green meadow, Collado Ventoso (the Windy Col) *(3)*. This is a delightful spot at which the landscape makes a dramatic change, opening out as you leave the forest and now with views to the south.

- Collado Ventoso is one of the two cols at the head of the Fuenfria valley, which contains some good walks described elsewhere in this collection. For this walk, from Collado Ventoso you should ascend fairly steeply up a slope to the south. This is not exactly a path, but it is a broad area of well-trodden land with exposed tree roots, heading towards a granite peak high above. The route makes an ascent of 150 metres to the base of the peak *(4)*, which is the first of six summits along the main ridge.

- On reaching the ridge, turn right and follow a good footpath, traversing along the crest of the hill, with a

LOS SIETE PICOS (THE SEVEN PEAKS)

series of rocky peaks above to the right. There are six main summits, and you may be able to reach one or two of them, depending on your own scrambling ability. Being granite there are few hand-holds, so you must take care, and you do this at your own risk.

- The very first summit is accessible with some difficulty. I can't give you an exact route, but in general terms go up a divide between the two main outcrops and then scramble up to the right. The highest and most accessible peak is the final one, at an altitude of 2,138 metres. There is a triangulation post on top, and on popular days you will see people up there. I can't describe the exact route, but generally it is best to approach it from the north-eastern side. Once more, if you go for it, take care as there are few handholds.

- Whether you go for the summits or not, simply follow the path from west to east all the way along the crest of the hill. Immediately beyond the last of the high peaks the path starts to descend, and you will find that the path separates on numerous occasions, but each time it comes together again.

- Just keep going downhill to the east and you will be fine. Soon you will reach a lower ridge, where a track skirts the northern flank of a hill with a transmitter on top (Cerro del Telegrafo). Follow the track, now going north-east, and it will bring you out on to the higher levels of a ski slope with a chair lift. Follow the line of the chair lift downhill, and at the bottom you can exit the ski piste on the left, via a gate in the fence, to return to the start of the walk.

WALK NO. 13

APPROXIMATE GPS WAYPOINTS (UTM):

1	Start and finish	415339 4515746
2	Camino Schmid	414864 4516045
3	Collado Ventoso	411793 4515850
4	Base of the first peak	411970 4515256

On the Siete Picos Ridge - **WALK 13**

PUERTO DE FUENRIA AND SENDA HERREROS

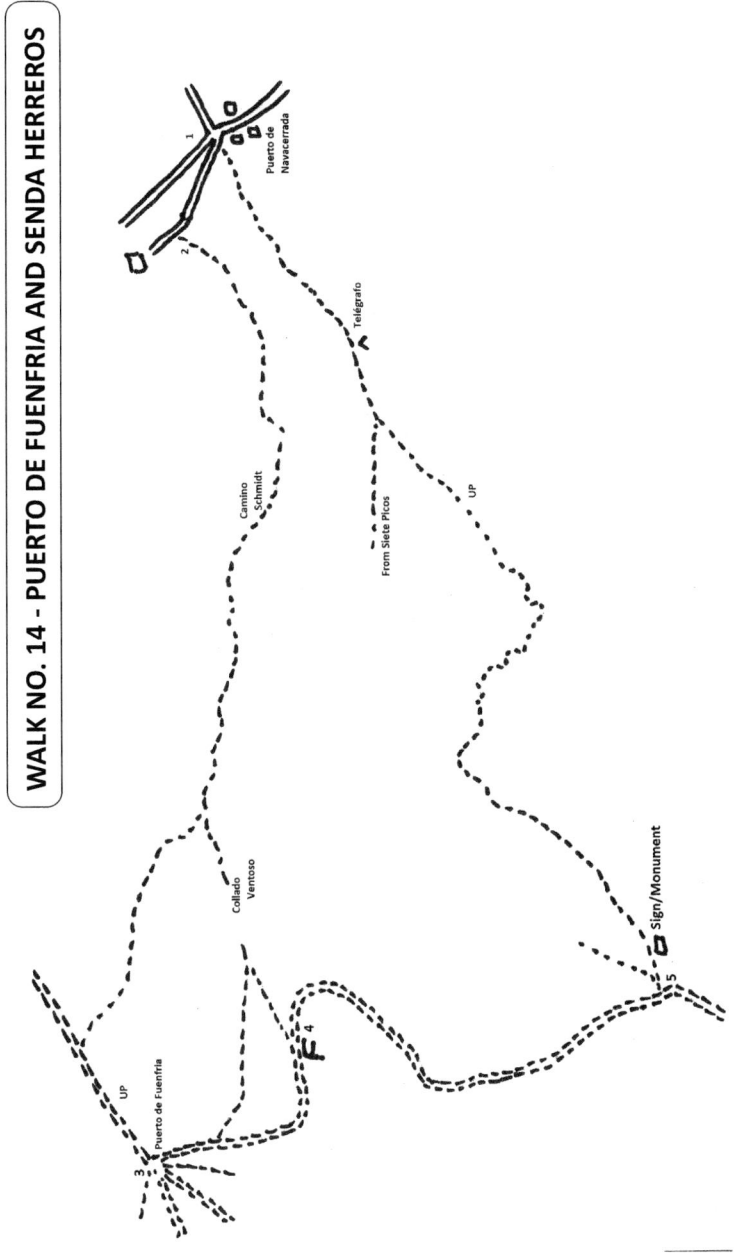

WALK NO. 14

PUERTO DE FUENFRIA AND SENDA HERREROS

Distance	16.5 km
Ascent	650 metres
Overall grade	Strenuous
Terrain	Footpaths, good tracks, boulders and some tree roots
Exposure	None
Highest point	1,975 metres

A circuit starting along the easy 'Camino Schmid', reaching a well-known col on the ancient route from Madrid to Segovia, crossing a pilgrims' route to Santiago de Compostela, and returning on the more demanding 'Senda Herreros'.

The first 3 kilometres of this walk are identical to Walk 13, but the rest of the route is longer, more difficult and over different terrain.

- The walk begins at the Puerto de Navacerrada, on the M601, at the top of the hill on the border between the provinces of Madrid and Segovia. In winter this is a ski resort, and there is a large car park. It can also be reached by the mountain train from the town of Cercedilla. Timetables are on www.renfe.es.

- Start the walk at the crest of the hill on the main road *(1)*. At the crossroads take a tarmac lane leading northwest. There is a fenced-off ski slope above to your left. Follow the lane and you will soon see signs for the 'Camino Schmid'. After half a kilometre you will see a military building ahead, and the Camino Schmid trail goes into the Scots pine woods to the left. Follow this easy path *(2)*, which is well marked with paint on the trees, and although I hesitate to use the term, you can't really go wrong.

- The Scots pines provide shade in hot weather, but due to their high-level foliage they permit light to enter and there are views to the north. The forest makes for very nice walking. If you are here at the weekend you will find plenty of other walkers.

- The path crosses a ski piste. If there is still snow on the ground it can be slippery, so take care. After about 3 kilometres you will reach a fork in the path. Take the right fork, following signs for the Senda de los Cospes and Puerto de Fuenfria. After a further 2 kilometres, the path joins a track coming up from below on the right. Follow it slightly uphill to the left and very soon you will join the long-distance path GR 10.1 (a variation on the main GR10). The track leads you very quickly to the Fuenfria pass *(3)* at the top of the hill. It is an open area, with some fences to protect new plantation. It was at one time a major crossroads, before the present roads were built. Going south from here are several paths and dirt roads, including a Roman footpath.

- For our route, take the main track on the left-hand (east) side of the valley, and follow it for 240 metres, to where a footpath goes up to the left *(**GPS users see footnote).* You have a choice here. You may continue to walk down the dirt road for a further kilometre of easy walking (with some good views on the way) or for more interest you can follow the footpath, which swings left, following the slopes of the hill above, until after 1.4 kilometres it joins a major path, on which you can turn right and walk down to the track you were on a few minutes ago. The path joins the track at a *fuente (4)*.

- From the *fuente*, continue to walk down the dirt road for a further 2.5 kilometres, to reach an open area, the Pradera de Navarrulaque *(5)*, which makes a great place for a break.

- At the Pradera, go to the east side of the open area and look for a wooden structure, which is a monument to Enrique Herreros, after whom the following footpath is named. (Evidently Herreros was into just about everything, including mountaineering.) Take the footpath which passes this monument, and follow it at first easily on the level, but soon ascending and becoming increasingly difficult. The tendency is north-east, and the path is marked with cairns and with yellow and white markers. It is vital to look for these as otherwise you will certainly lose the path. The next hour of the walk is mainly uphill and is tricky to navigate, with the path taking unexpected turns and crossing exposed tree roots, boulders and sloping granite slabs. In case you lose the path, here are a couple of UTM GPS references to get you back on course: 413108 4514500 and 413223 4514660. The tricky section lasts for about a kilometre. If you lose the yellow and white marks, go back and find them again.

- The path begins to contour, although still with some ups and downs, and then joins the main path coming down from the Siete Picos (Walk 13). Turn right, and when the ground levels and opens out, keep to the right (there are several tracks to the left) and cross the top of Peña Hueca, a rocky hilltop at 1,946 metres. Continue on the path to the top of Cerro del Telegrafo (1,978 metres), which involves a bit of a boulder scramble, and then pass by the smaller Alto del Telegrafo, with a statue of an angel on its summit. Continue from there on broad tracks to reach the top of two ski lifts, and descend via the right-hand one, go through a narrow opening in the fence on the left at the bottom, and you will be back at the start of the walk.

PUERTO DE FUENFRIA AND SENDA HERREROS

APPROXIMATE GPS WAYPOINTS (UTM):

1	Start and finish	415387 4515804
2	Camino Schmid	414864 4516045
3	Puerto de Fuenfria	410582 4516240
4	Fuente	411115 4515581
5	Pradera	411313 4513665

**Footnote for GPS Users.

The Alpina GPS map shows the path referred to in the walk description, but it is in the wrong place. If following GPS, do not turn left where Alpina indicates, but walk on for a further 80 metres to find the path.

La Ventana - **WALK 17**

WALK NO. 15

WALK NO. 15 AND 15A - LAS CANCHAS AND PEÑA PINTADA

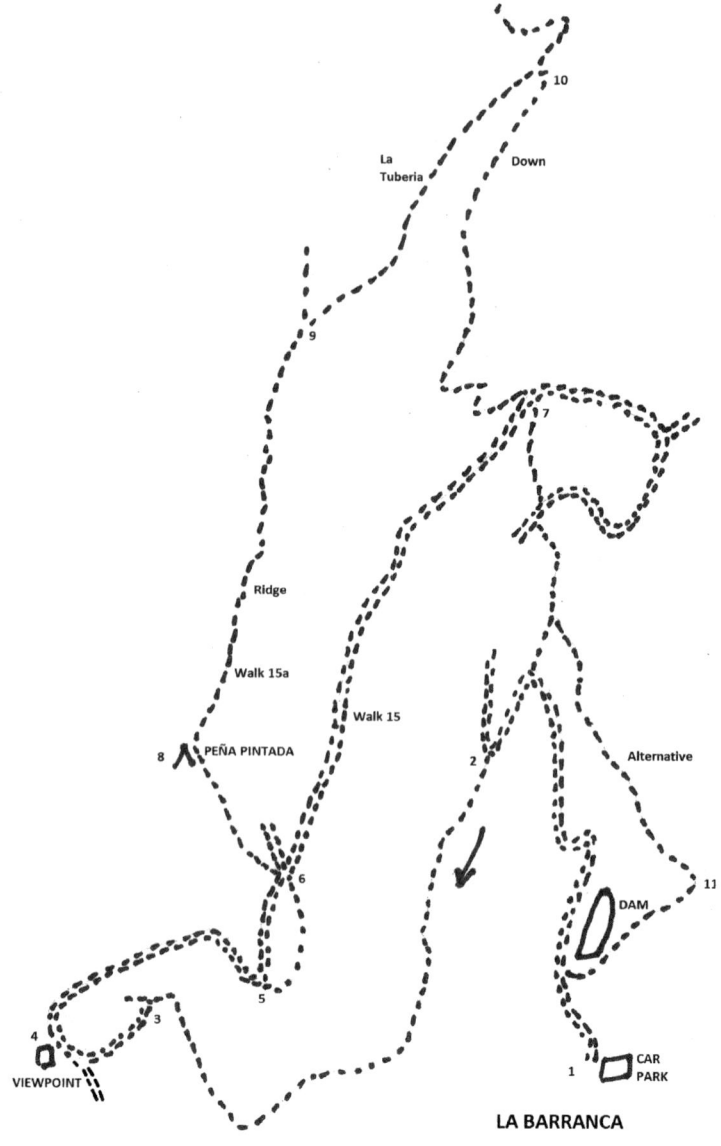

WALK NO. 15

MIRADOR DE LAS CANCHAS

Distance	10 kilometres
Ascent	390 metres
Overall grade	Easy
Terrain	Good, generally level dirt tracks and footpaths
Exposure	None
Highest point	1,742 metres

An easy walk, almost entirely on good surfaces and with only gradual inclines. Although the walk is largely through delightful Scots pine woods, it brings brilliant views, the highpoint of Las Canchas being memorable.

- The walk begins at the car park at La Barranca, outside the small town of Navacerrada. Driving on the M607 from Madrid, shortly after a roundabout on the edge of Navacerrada, and just after the kilometre 57 sign, take a right turn signposted: Parque de Bomberos and La Barranca. The narrow but well-surfaced road goes on for about 2.5 kilometres and there is a car park on the right *(1)*.

- Leaving the car park, walk up the track going north, passing two small reservoirs immediately on your right. Stay on the track, which takes a sharp turn to the left, passing by a tree-walk set-up called 'Pino a Pino'. Stay on the track as it swings right again. Our route follows the track, but you can leave the track and walk a short distance alongside the river bed to the right, a very nice area. But join the track again after only 250 metres. You will then arrive at a junction, where yellow and white paint indicates a route going straight ahead. But ignore it. That is not our route. Instead, swing to the left.

- After another 150 metres, the track swings to the right again, but you should take a footpath going straight ahead to the south *(2)*. The path ascends very slightly, going round the end of a hillside for about 2 kilometres. The route goes through the woods all the way, but the thin pines give views to the south, and particularly of the Navacerrada reservoir below. After 2 kilometres on the path you will reach a junction *(3)*, where you should keep to the left-hand, lower track. Shortly after this junction you will reach a more important junction, where you should turn right on a broad dirt road. Very soon on the left you will reach a rocky viewpoint *(4)*, with a noticeboard pointing out the things you can see.

- Continue up the dirt road, and very soon you will see some more notices away to your right, on the site of a demolished sanatorium. Unfortunately, the views here are now obscured by the bushes which have inconsiderately grown since the signs were erected! Continue on the track, now going generally east. At a sharp left-hand bend *(5)* you can leave the track again on its right-hand side and take a footpath, which follows the same general line as the track. The path is marked with cairns, and leads you to the Canchas viewpoint *(6)*, with stunning views across to the peaks of Bola del Mundo and La Maliciosa.

- From the Mirador (viewpoint) continue north on the dirt track, now downhill, for 1.5 kilometres. Just before it swings right and crosses a bridge, take a path down to the right-hand side *(7)*. It has the ubiquitous yellow and white paint marks from time to time. If you miss this path, don't worry, just stay on the track and turn right at the next junction and you will reach the same point, via a slightly longer route.

- Assuming that you in fact do find the path, after 300 metres downhill, it meets the track again. Go a few metres down the track and then the path starts again on the left-hand side. Follow the path for half a kilometre, and you will reach a bend in the main track, which you walked up earlier. Follow this track back down to the car park.

APPROXIMATE GPS WAYPOINTS (UTM):

1	Start and finish	416163 4511610
2	Footpath	415918 4512747
3	Left fork	414856 4511883
4	Viewpoint	414716 4511746
5	Start of path	415256 4511924
6	Las Canchas viewpoint	415287 4512256
7	Path to the right	416018 4513668

Cancho de la Cabeza - **WALK 30**

WALK NO. 15A

MIRADOR DE LAS CANCHAS AND PEÑA PINTADA

Distance	14 km
Ascent	680 metres
Overall grade	Moderate
Terrain	good dirt tracks and footpaths
Exposure	None
Highest point	1,883 metres

This walk is a longer, higher and more strenuous variation on Walk 15. It goes to the viewpoint at Las Canchas as in Walk 15 then ascends to traverse a broad ridge, before descending to join the latter parts of the other walk once more.

For the first part of this walk, follow the instructions for the first part of Walk 15 as far as the Las Canchas viewpoint. The numeric GPS references continue the sequence of Walk 15.

- From the viewpoint *(6)*, ignore the main track going downhill to the north, and also ignore a path going up at a tangent to the left side of the main track. Instead, take a path directly uphill to the north-west. The path ascends the 'nose' of the hill, and after only half a kilometre, reaches the summit of Peña Pintada, at 1,851 metres altitude *(8)*.

- Turn right, and go north along the top of the ridge for about 1.25 kilometres. Then take a right fork *(9)* and follow a path leading along the eastern slopes of the hill. There is an old water pipe running along the path, for which reason this route is named 'La Tubería' (roughly translated as 'the Tubes'). The path follows the contour for a while then climbs slightly until, 1 kilometre from where you joined this path, you reach a T-junction. Going straight ahead would lead you to the Puerto de Navacerrada, but instead of that, turn sharp right *(10)* on the path going down and back to the right.

- Follow the path down as it zigzags through woods until it meets a broad dirt track. At this point you reach a broad track at waypoint 7 of walk 15 *(7)*.

- When you reach this broad track, the path continues downhill almost directly opposite. There are yellow and white paint marks from time to time. After 300 metres downhill, you will meet the track again. Go a few metres to the right on the track and then the path starts to descend again. Follow the path for half a kilometre and you will reach a bend in the main track, which you walked up earlier. You can follow this track back down to the car park, but for an attractive end to the walk you can keep to the left bank of the stream and follow a path down to the right, which will lead you to a point looking down on to the reservoirs near the start of the walk *(11)*. Follow this path down to the dam across the reservoir (a lovely spot), cross the dam and turn left, back to the car park.

APPROXIMATE GPS WAYPOINTS (UTM):

6	Las Canchas viewpoint	415287 4512256
7	Broad track	416018 4513668
8	Peña Pintada	415065 4512634
9	Path to the right	415362 4513853
10	Sharp right turn	416036 4514607
11	Above the reservoirs	416427 4512242

WALK NO. 16

WALK NO. 16 - LA MALICIOSA

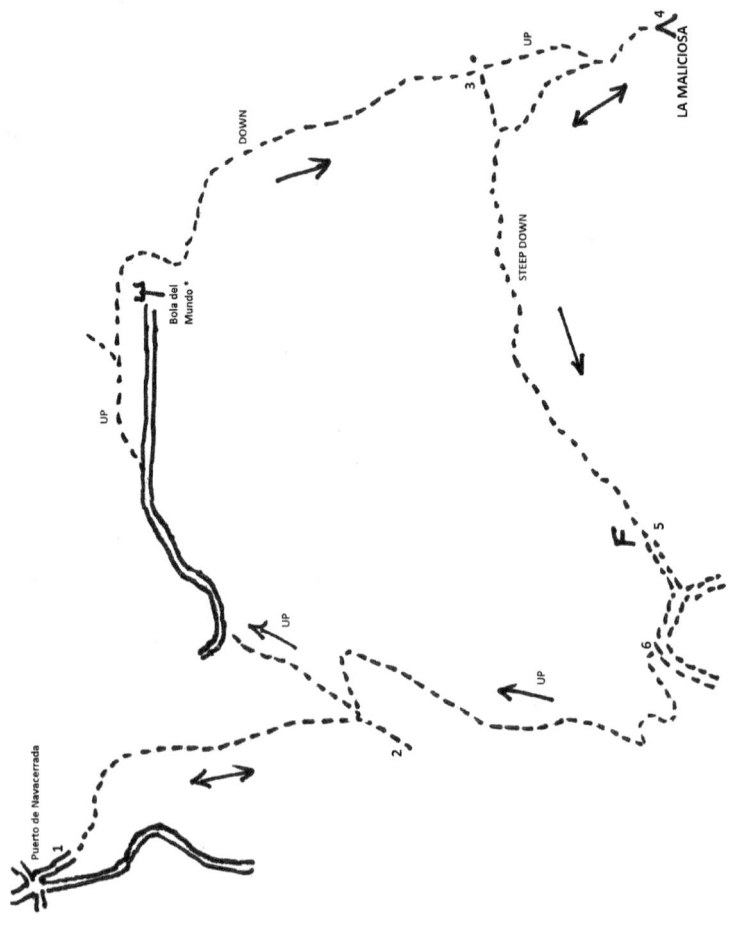

WALK NO. 16

BOLA DEL MUNDO, LA MALICIOSA AND FUENTE DE LA CAMPANILLA

Distance	14 km
Ascent	950 metres
Overall grade	Strenuous
Terrain	Tracks and footpaths (some loose)
Exposure	None
Highest point	2,250 metres

A circular walk passing Madrid's radio transmitters, ascending to the spectacular peak of La Malicosa, and then returning via a lower level route with great views.

A dominant feature of the hills to the north of Madrid, are the enormous radio transmitters at Bola del Mundo (which is also known as Alto de la Guarramillas). The antennae can be seen for miles around. This walk goes up to the transmitters, and then gives relatively easy access to the high peak of La Maliciosa. (More difficult ascents of the latter are described in Walks 17 and 18.)

- The walk begins at Puerto de Navacerrada, a ski resort at the highest point of the M601, which links Madrid to Segovia. Park at the Puerto, an unsightly place with wire fences and ski lifts. There is a large car park at the top of the pass.

- At the top of the pass the main road from the south swings left and a right turn leads to Rascafria. But just before the Rascafria road, and immediately before the enormous car park, a minor road goes south-east below a ski lift. It passes a 'Cruz Roja' (Red Cross) building. Walk up this road *(1)*. Go past the right- hand side of the ski lift and pass through a gate. Follow a good track gently uphill going south-east. After 1.4 kilometres the path swings sharp left, but first it is worth taking a look at the view from the rocky area ahead *(2)*, then return to follow the original path uphill. It reaches a road. Follow it uphill to reach the top station of a chair lift. Cross to the far side of the road and turn right on a footpath going parallel with the road, which will now be above on your right. The road goes all the way to Bola del Mundo, but the footpath is more interesting. As you near the transmitters, leave the path and walk straight up to the radio station perimeter.

- From the transmitters, follow a good and well-walked footpath leading at first just east of south, then veering to the south, and losing about 180 metres altitude. After 1.5 kilometres you will pass a junction of paths, where a rain gauge stands at the bottom of a dip at Collado del Piornal *(3)*. You will return to this point later. But for now, continue on the popular path to the south-east, making an easy ascent to the summit of La Maliciosa *(4)*.

- The rocky summit has plenty of interest and great views all round. There is a lot of potential scrambling if you choose to spend time here, and there are several walking routes from the summit. But for this walk, return the way you came, towards Bola del Mundo, for just less than a kilometre to Collado del Piornal *(3)*. From there, take the path down to the left (west) and descend on a path alongside a watercourse. The path is eroded, loose and difficult, and I find it easier at times to leave the path and walk on the grass alongside the watercourse. The path and the watercourse stay close together, so you can judge for yourself. Halfway down the hill the path splits, but these are branches of the same path and come back together again. Keep going down for about 2 kilometres from the col. You will enter woods, where the going is easier, and then you will encounter a large *fuente*, with picnic benches, a very good place for a rest. This is Fuente de la Campanilla *(5)*.

- From the *fuente*, a broad track continues descending, and very shortly it joins a broad dirt road. Turn right along this road. It crosses a bridge and swings left. Just round the bend, look for metal plates nailed to the trees on the right and painted yellow and white *(6)*. They mark the path back to Puerto de Navacerrada. Follow this path uphill through the woods, with views opening up as you ascend. You can see quite clearly La Maliciosa and the whole route of the descent you have just made. Continue on the path as it gradually ascends high to the left side of a valley.

- There are very few, if any, alternatives along this path until it swings to the left and meets another path (La Tuberia – see Walk 15a). Turn right here and soon the path swings to the left and reaches the ridge close to the viewpoint *(2)* mentioned earlier. Turn right here and stroll down the path back to the start.

APPROXIMATE GPS WAYPOINTS (UTM)

1	Minor road	415397 4515781
2	Viewpoint	415803 4514605
3	Collado del Piornal	417954 4514161
4	La Maliciosa	418252 4513356
5	Fuente de la Campanilla	416321 4513577
6	Path to the right	416018 4513668

WALK NO. 17

WALK NO. 17 - LA MALICIOSA FROM LA BARRANCA

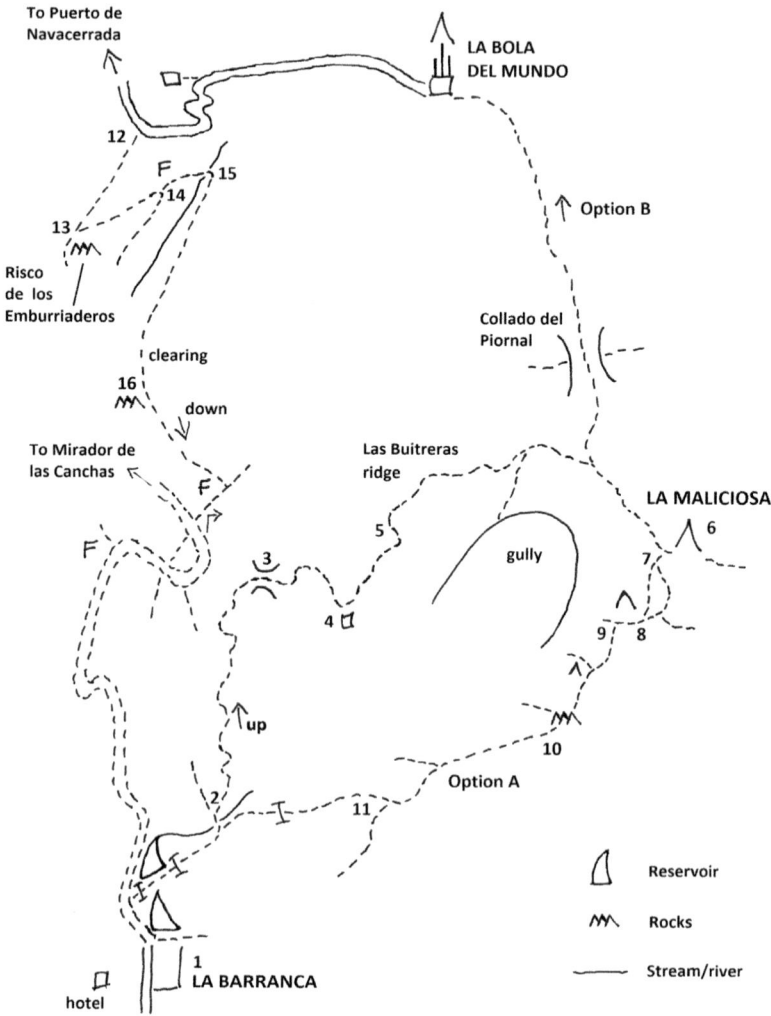

WALK NO. 17

LA BARRANCA TO LA MALICIOSA VIA CUERDA DE LAS BUITERERAS

Distance	12 km or 15 km
Ascent	900 metres or 1,050 metres
Overall grade	Strenuous
Terrain	Paths and boulders, some scrambling
Exposure	A couple of short scrambles up rock, no significant exposure
Highest point	La Maliciosa: 2,227 metres, La Bola del Mundo: 2,262

This route to La Maliciosa from La Barranca is one of the least used but one of the most interesting as it runs along the base of Las Buitreras ridge. It is slightly longer than other options as it will have you scrambling up short sections of rock, but offers unimpeded views over the valley.

The walk also offers two options for returning: one (Option A below) via the steep south slope and past El Peñotillo Alto, the other (Option B) via a more unconventional route along Arroyo de Peña Cabrita. Option B is the longer route, and covers similar ground to parts of Walk 16. Option A is shorter, but covers completely different ground.

- The starting point is the popular car park of La Barranca. One hundred metres past the km 57 marker on the M-607, take a sharp right turn, signposted: Parque de Bomberos and De Pino a Pino. Drive up the road for 2.5 km until you reach a series of car parks on the right. The starting point is at the furthest car park, just before a reservoir *(1)*.

- From the car park, walk up the main track. Ignore a gate to the first reservoir on the right. Continue past the barrier on the broad track and after 150 metres, pass through a gate on the right (it has a 'No Swimming' sign on it). Pass a small building with a sign for Casa de Guias de Navacerrada and cross the walkway over the second reservoir.

- As you pass through the gate on the far side of the walkway, you will see a path heading straight ahead through the forest. Stay on that path (it actually forks at one point but the resulting two paths converge again) for approximately 500 metres as it swings left and drops down to a stream (ignore the path that heads right, parallel to the stream).

- Cross the stream and up the bank on the other side, then swing right *(2)* onto a steep ascending path through the trees. You will see cairns and occasionally faded white/green markings on rocks as the path rises up to a series of viewpoints at increasing altitude.

- One kilometre after starting to climb, the path levels out at a small col, where you will be able to see the radio masts at Bola del Mundo. Head right (east) across the clearing until you come to a rock face where some cairns mark the ascent. Here you will have a short scramble up the rock *(3)*.

- At the top, follow cairns (and faded white/green stripes) on a path over and around rocks. The cairns suddenly swing upwards to the left and, after a short ascent, swing back to the right onto a clearer path. The cairned path heads to the right of the large rock face ahead. You will eventually see the rock 'window' of La Ventana above to the right. Follow the cairns/stripes up to La Ventana *(4)*. Pass through it for a view of the Madrid plateau below and the peak of La Maliciosa, the highest peak to the east on the opposite side of the valley.

- You will see cairns next to the rock face to the left, heading north-east along the Las Buitreras ridge. Follow that rocky path, on a steady upward trajectory along (although not on top of) the ridge. At one stage, the cairns swing up to the left and reach a small col, where you can again see the radio masts. Look to the rocks on the right and the cairns take you on a short scramble *(5)*, but nothing excessively difficult and with little exposure (however, immediately after the scramble it's possible to climb up left onto the top of the ridge itself if you so wish).

- Continue to follow the cairned path until the Las Buitreras ridge meets the ridge to the west (the left as you see it) of La Maliciosa peak. The cairns lead you around the back and on top of the La Maliciosa ridge (2.2 km from La Ventana). At the top of that ridge you will meet the main path (marked with painted white/yellow stripes) ascending from Collado del Piornal. Continue to the east to the summit of La Maliciosa *(6)*.

- There are numerous routes back to La Barranca. Here are two options:

- ***Option A (the shorter option with the least altitude gain, but with a much steeper descent):***

- From the peak, look down to the south and you will see the large secondary peak of El Peñotillo (also referred to as El Peñotillo Alto) just below, separated by a large gully. That's the gully you will be heading into now. To do so, return from the summit and retrace your steps for about 25 metres along the path. Now swing left over the top of the ridge *(7)* and start heading into the gully. There is a large rock field in the middle of the gully, so your main choices for descending it are the converging cairned paths that run to the left or to right of the rocks. It's easier going on the left-hand side (directly below the Maliciosa peak, so aim for a wooden post below and continue to follow the cairns down along the rocks), but the right offers the possibility of an interesting scramble up El Peñotillo. Whichever you choose, continue descending loose rock until you start to come level with the lower base of El Peñotillo, which is when you must start to make your way over to the right-hand side of the gully.

- When you reach the base, you will find cairns that mark a path that hugs the vertical south-facing rock face underneath El Peñotillo (*8*). Continue along the cairned path for approximately 250 metres and look down the steep slope left for cairns that mark the path down (*9*) (There are a few cairns scattered among the rocks, but the GPS location indicates the best route down.) As you look below to the south-west, you will notice a line of rocky outcrops (this is the ridge of Cuerda de los Almorchones) and the La Barranca car park in the distance beyond. You are ultimately aiming for the clear path that you can see running below the outcrops, in the direction of the car park. The initial descent from the rock face is steep and rocky, but soon swings around right and levels out considerably as it descends towards the ridge. When you are on that much better path, continue downwards underneath El Peñotillo Bajo and other rocky outcrops, ignoring any paths to the right tempting you upwards and over the ridge. After 800 metres, the path will eventually reach some rocks. Navigate your way through the rocks following the cairns, and then turn right, through the fallen fence (*10*). The path is slightly sketchier here, but there are plenty of cairns to mark the way down.

- After approximately 300 metres, the path levels out onto a kind of plateau and cairns mark a couple of different options (*11*); cairns marking a path directly in the direction of La Barranca car park that you can see on the left or cairns marking a path heading for the treeline slightly to the right. Both will get you back. Taking the right-hand (straight) option, the path will enter the treeline and pass through a gate. Continue on the path straight, ignoring a tangent to a stream on the right, until you emerge from the trees at the walkway over the reservoir that you crossed earlier.

- ***Option B (the longer option for distance and with greater altitude gain, but the descent is mostly easier).***

- From La Maliciosa return to the well-trodden path marked with cairns and white/yellow stripes along the ridge, which swings right and zigzags down to Collado del Piornal. When you arrive at the col, you'll see a rain gauge there – a small metal tripod-like structure and marked on maps as *pluviómetro*. Continue straight on, ascending the path with white/yellow markings towards the masts on the top of La Bola del Mundo (Alto de las Guarramillas). Once there, make your way to the far side of the masts and descend down the concrete road heading west. You will pass El Bola Bar, a cafeteria (and top of the ski lift) with wonderful views but somewhat unpredictable opening hours. After 1.4 km, on a sharp right-hand bend, the white/yellow stripes leave the track and go left onto a path *(12)*.

- Follow the marked rocky path down the hill and, just as you reach the rocks of Risco de los Emburriaderos, swing sharp left *(13)* onto a descending path – also marked with white/yellow stripes, running east. The marked path soon swings sharp right *(14)*. However, ignore the bend and continue straight, onto a path that runs past Fuente de la Caña (called Fuente de Peña Cabrita on some maps). Follow some cairns as they make their way gradually down to the gully of Arroyo de Peña Cabrita on your right, and then cross the stream. As soon as you cross, head right along the stream and follow the cairns *(15)* as they run parallel to it. This path slowly descends along the gully south, and then gradually pulls away from the stream.

- The path runs through the forest and you will ultimately reach a large clearing, where the cairns suddenly disappear. Keeping to the right-hand side of the clearing, and without losing altitude, cross it towards the rocks to the south. Among the rocks, next to a flat rock viewpoint, you will find a large cairn and white/green painted stripes *(16)*. Follow the rocky cairned path as it descends from there. A little further down there's a steep section with a lot of loose rock, which can be slippery – nothing dangerous, you just have to watch your footing. The path also gets somewhat sketchy here, but is marked with cairns, albeit intermittently. Once you have passed this section, the path levels out and you suddenly emerge from the trees behind Fuente de la Campanilla. Cross the river to the *fuente* and then head down the broad path right; after a short distance you come to a crossing with a broad track, with a wooden sign and a stone obelisk. Continue straight across on to the path on the other side and follow it for a short distance until you meet the broad dirt track again. Turn right and follow the track 2 km back to the main car park.

APPROXIMATE GPS REFERENCES (UTM)

1	La Barranca car park	416170 4511756
2	Turn off right after stream	416419 4512262
3	Scramble up	416653 4513239
4	La Ventana	416950 4513175
5	Small col and scramble	417161 4513513
6	La Maliciosa summit	418256 4513364
7	Option A: Step over ridge left into gully	418235 4513379

LA BARRANCA TO LA MALICIOSA VIA CUERDA DE LAS BUITERERAS

8	Option A: Cairns hugging Peñotillo rock face	418031 4512960
9	Option A: Start descending left	417823 4512948
10	Option A: Through fence right	417317 4512389
11	Option A: Take right fork towards trees	417014 4512354
12	Option B: Left turn off concrete track	416179 4515119
13	Option B: Turn left, following white/yellow stripes	415915 4514696
14	Option B: Continue straight	416174 4514778
15	Option B: Path on other side of river	416315 4514747
16	Option B: Cairn at far end of clearing. Path down.	416285 4514098

La Ventana - **WALK 17**

WALK NO. 18

WALK NO. 18 - LA MALICIOSA FROM BECERRIL DE LA SIERRA

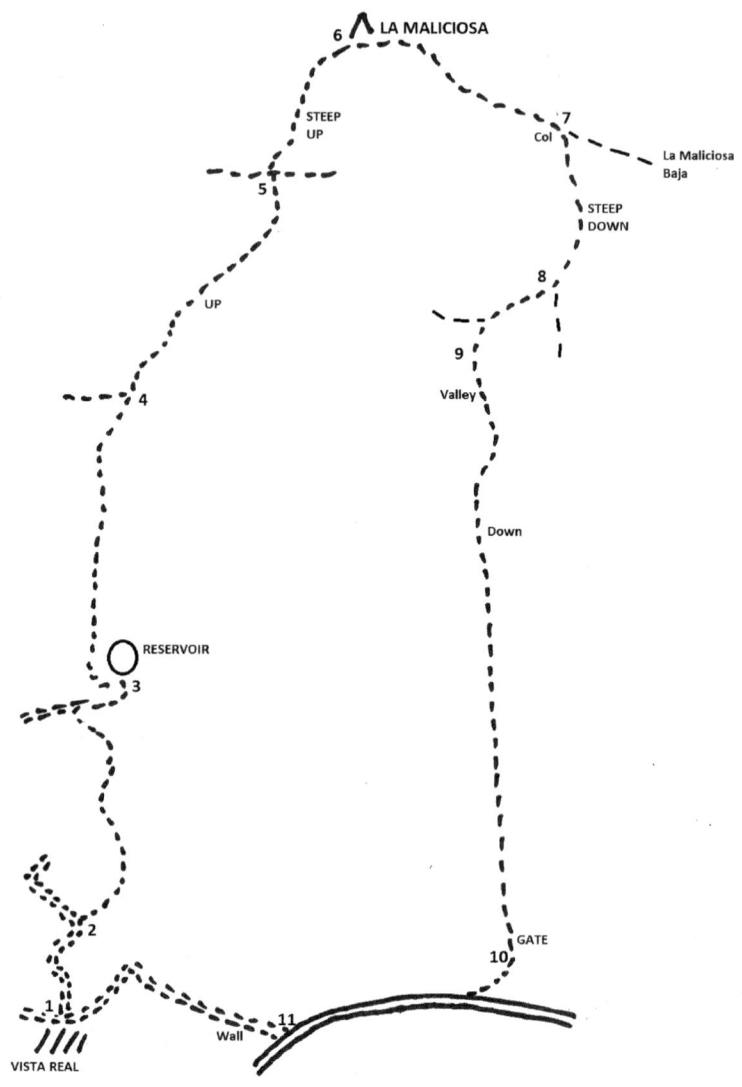

WALK NO. 18

ASCENT OF LA MALICIOSA (2,227 metres) FROM BECERRIL DE LA SIERRA

Distance	14 km
Ascent	1,170 metres
Overall grade	Strenuous
Terrain	Good tracks and footpaths, and a steep, rocky descent
Exposure	Virtually none
Highest point	2,227 metres

A direct ascent of the major peak overlooking the small town of Becerril de la Sierra.

The name of the mountain translates into English as the 'Malicious One'. But it is a beautiful hill, and it is one of the most prominent peaks of the central system.

- The walk begins at the top of the housing estate of Vista Real, to the north side of the M607 highway on the outskirts of Becerril. There is ample car parking at the top of the estate.

- Walk uphill to the highest level of the estate. Go through a gate *(1)* and walk up a track going north. The track zig-zags but you can cut out the bends on short footpaths. After 600 metres on the track, where it swings sharp left, a footpath *(2)* goes straight ahead. Take this path. It leads gradually uphill for 1 kilometre, and rejoins the broad track you left earlier as it levels off. Turn right on the track, and when it almost immediately swings to the left, go straight on through a gate. From here a path leads you within 250 metres to a reservoir, the Embalse de la Maliciosa *(3)*. Turn left to skirt the south side and then the west side of the reservoir, and at the far north-west corner look for a footpath going uphill to the north, and through a gate. Take this path.

- The route is easy to follow now as it makes straight for the mountain to the north, but for now keeping to the floor of the valley. An open, green section makes a nice spot for a few minutes rest. A little farther on, a path goes away to the left *(4)*, but ignore it and keep straight ahead. The path is now heading in a north-easterly direction, and starts to ascend more steeply. You will pass by some rocky outcrops, and there are some zigzags in the path, but that apart you can't really go wrong.

- As you get to the higher reaches of the hill, at an altitude of 1,931 metres, you will cross another path *(5)*. The high rock outcrop of El Penotillo is above you on your left. It can be a little confusing here, but go straight across the path at the junction, and continue north to north-east, keeping El Penotillo to your left.

- The path becomes increasingly steep and crosses loose boulders and rough scree. This section is much more strenuous, but continue as best you can, always ascending. You will do this more by intuition than by following a defined path. You will soon reach the summit *(6)*, where there are great views in all directions, and good rocky areas provide comfortable places for a picnic.

- From the summit of La Maliciosa, descend on the path heading east, marked with the white/yellow markings of the route PRM16. The path zigzags down the slope for 1 km to Collado de las Vacas (the Cows' Col), which lies between La Maliciosa and La Maliciosa Baja. Cross the col following the white/yellow markings and, just before the path starts to ascend on the far side of the col, look for cairns to your right between two large rocks *(7)*. These lead to a cairned path that will take you on a steep descent into the valley that stretches away to the south.

- After approximately 800 metres of descent, the cairns veer sharply to the right, although the path appears to continue straight ahead. Follow the cairns to the right *(8)*. The path drops directly down towards the valley floor. After a further 400 metres, the path reaches the bottom of the valley and crosses a stream and pool (or dry riverbed in summer). Here swing left onto a path that runs south, parallel to the river along the bottom of the valley *(9)*. (Swinging right would return you to the summit of La Maliciosa.)

- Continue on that path along the valley bottom, with the river on your left, for 3 km. As the path widens at the end, you will eventually arrive at a metal gate. Pass through the gate and follow the path as it bends round to the right *(10)*, and after 300 metres you will meet a road. Here you will start to see the yellow arrows of the Madrid section of the Camino de Santiago and white/red markings of GR10. Continue right, down the path, parallel to the road. After approximately 700 metres, the path veers right along a wall *(11)*, leaving the road behind. Continue up the path following yellow Camino de Santiago arrows until it becomes a larger dirt track, swinging left. Continue following the markings, ignoring a gate into a street to the left, and you will soon arrive at the gate you passed through at the beginning to return to your starting point in Vista Real.

APPROXIMATE GPS WAYPOINTS (UTM)

1	Gate at start and finish	417243 4509469
2	Footpath	417287 4509915
3	Reservoir	417362 4510770
4	Ignore path to the left	417520 4512022
5	Path junction at 1,931 metres	418075 4512890

WALK NO. 18

6	Summit	418352 4513443
7	Turn off from Collado de las Vacas	419165 4513145
8	Cairns take a sharp right turn	419182 4512449
9	River crossing and left turn	418960 4512401
10	Turn off onto Camino/GR10 after gate	418996 4509675
11	Turn right away from road	418085 4509431

La Maliciosa - **WALKS 16 to 18**

SIERRA DE LOS PORRONES AND CHARCA VERDE

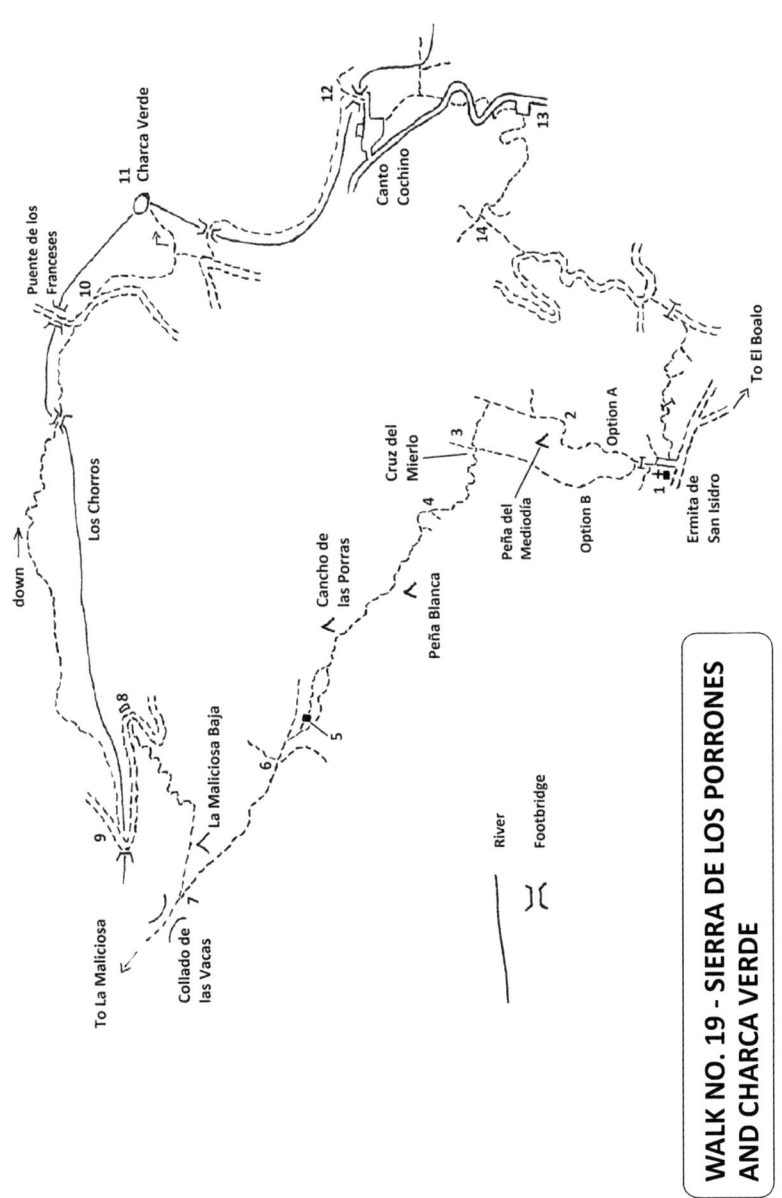

WALK NO. 19 - SIERRA DE LOS PORRONES AND CHARCA VERDE

WALK NO. 19

SIERRA DE LOS PORRONES AND CHARCA VERDE

Distance	24 km
Ascent	1,200 metres
Overall grade	Very strenuous
Terrain	Tracks and footpaths
Exposure	Exposed on the clavijas, but none otherwise
Highest point	La Maliciosa Baja: 1,938 metres

A walk up the broad ridge of Cuerda de los Porrones, offering some of the best views of La Pedriza. One option includes a short ascent on *clavijas* (iron rods embedded in the rock to help you up a vertical and exposed section of rock) and the walk also visits the popular natural pool of Charca Verde.

The Cuerda de los Porrones is a large ridge that runs along the south-western edge of La Pedriza, up to La Maliciosa peak at its western end. The walk climbs its southern flank by the Senda de las Cabras, a steep and exciting ascent that includes a short but vertical climb on *clavijas* (but there is an option to avoid this). It then continues up to La Maliciosa Baja – one of the best viewpoints over the park – before winding down through La Pedriza's gullies alongside the Manzanares river. Due to vulture nesting season, the Senda de las Cabras can only be used from August to December. Therefore, to do the walk outside those months, or if you want to avoid the *clavijas* (the pins), use the alternative outward route.

- The walk starts at the car park next to Ermita de San Isidro (also called Ermita de El Boalo), a small hermitage and marvellous picnic area at the foot of the Torreta de los Porrones. The closest village is El Boalo. In the centre of the village there's a roundabout with a cross in the middle; from there turn onto Avenida de los Prados, then immediately left onto Calle del Vallejuelo, followed by the 3rd right onto Calle Cañada. This street soon turns into a dirt road. Continue until you reach another large dirt road crossing left to right. Turn left; the Ermita is 100 metres up the road on your right. Park in the car park there.

- At the north-western corner of the car park *(1)*, at the opening in the wooden fence next to a gate, take the path heading up the hill straight towards the pointed peak above (Peña del Mediodía, also called Peña del Aguila) and start climbing. Ignore paths to the left and right. You soon come to a makeshift gate; pass through it.

- From here you have 2 options: (A) to head straight, which leads to the Senda de las Cabras and its *clavijas* (see footnote); or (B) to swing left onto a path that will avoid the *clavijas* (this is the route that must be used from January through to July).

- **Option A:** For the Senda de las Cabras, continue on the path straight up the hill. There are not many cairns at this stage (there are more the higher you get) so some intuition might be necessary, but make sure you stay on the path heading pretty much straight for Peña del Mediodía. You will soon need to scramble over some rocks. After you have climbed a while, and with the peak looming directly above you, you will need to scramble over a section of larger boulders. Then the path and increasingly frequent cairns start to veer slightly to the left, and ultimately lead to the left-hand side of Peña del Mediodía. As you reach the left side of the rock face, the cairns swing right – over and around boulders – and lead underneath large slabs of rock to the other side. As you emerge on the other side, you will see a steep gully descending to the south. The cairns swing left, upwards, to what looks like an unsurpassable rock wall. As you get closer, you will see metal rods embedded in the rock: the *clavijas (2)*. Use them to climb a 10-metre vertical section of the rock. Aided by the rods, it's not a difficult climb, but it is quite vertical and exposed.

- When you've completed the *clavijas*, continue on the cairned path up and over the top of Peña del Mediodía and you will suddenly see magnificent views over La Pedriza and the Cuerda Larga to the north. You will now start a gradual descent – ignore a path to the right – until you come to a fence and a '*Coto Privado de Caza*' (private hunting) sign; pass through the gap and immediately turn left onto a path running parallel to the fence. You will shortly come to another large gap in the fence on the left, between a small black/white sign and some rocks; pass through it – you are now at the Collado de Valdehalcones col *(3)* – and then turn right, making your way around the rocks. After about 10 metres, you will find a stone cross on the ground; this is the Cruz del Mierlo, steeped in legends of banditry for which the area was known. Continue westward (with the fence now on your right).

- **Option B:** Turn left after the gate and take the path as it gradually swings right around and then on top of the hump. As you do, you will see a gully that climbs steeply towards the col above you to the north. The path firstly descends to the river bed below at the foot of the gully and then climbs steeply. Continue up that steep path until you reach the col of Collado de Valdehalcones *(3)*. There's a cairned path crossing right to left before you reach a fence and the stone cross of Cruz del Mierlo on the ground in front of the rocks. Turn left onto that path westward.

- From Cruz del Mierlo, continue on the path, following cairns (you might also see faded red dots) as it gradually climbs over and around rocks. After about 1 km, you will come to a fork *(4)*; stay right. Soon after that there's another fork and again, stay right. Immediately after this second fork you will see a red dot on a rock to your left; confirmation you are on the correct path. The path then continues upward, with occasional easy scrambling required, until you pass underneath a rock. After you have done so, you will see the entire length of the Cuerda de los Porrones ridge, with its minor peaks, ending at La Maliciosa in the distance. Drop down to the cairned path you can see below and follow it for approximately 3 km along the ridge. Plenty of cairns and faded red dots lead the way and the path will take you past the rocky peaks of Peña Blanca and Cancho de las Porras. After that, the path splits into two, both of which are cairned. You may not even notice the split and both paths lead to the same place. You will eventually see a small rock shelter *(5)* to your right, after which the path starts to veer right. Very soon it converges with the large PR-M16 path (marked with white/yellow stripes) rising from the east.

- Now on the PR-M16, continue for a short distance until you reach Collado Porrón *(6)* – which, despite the name, does not really look like a col – marked with white/yellow stripes on a rock in the middle of the path. Ahead, up the same path, you will see the hump of La Maliciosa Baja, with rocky terrain on the left and forest on the right. Continue up the PR-M16 straight, up the rocky left-hand side of the hump.

- As the path levels out, it avoids climbing to the top of La Maliciosa Baja (which is above you to the right), instead skirting around to its left. As you complete this short section, you will soon look down onto Collado de la Vacas (the Cows' Col), the large col that separates La Maliciosa Baja (now behind you) and the much larger La Maliciosa peak in front.

- However, do not start descending to Collado de Las Vacas; you must look for cairns on a path *(7)* that cuts back to the right from the PR-M16 (the cairns start some 50 or so metres before the start of the descent to the col).

- That path takes you on a short ascent up to and along the flat top of La Maliciosa Baja, offering uninterrupted views of La Pedriza. The cairned path then swings left, heading down the broad ridge to the north-east, directly to the visible bend in a large dirt track far below. On that bend is Collado de los Pastores (the Shepherds' Col) *(8)*, another wonderful viewpoint over La Pedriza with information boards naming the surrounding peaks.

- From the viewpoint, head left down the large track. You will soon arrive at a sharp right-hand bend over the Puente de los Manchegos footbridge. Soon beyond the bend you will see a large cairn on the right marking a path that descends to the right *(9)*. Take that path, which is part of the PR-M18 and is therefore also marked with painted white/yellow stripes.

- The path descends gradually into the valley, initially in a straight line and then in increasingly steeper zigzags as it drops to the river; it also runs past Los Chorros, a series of waterfalls and pools that are only evident when there's significant water in the river. Approximately 3.5 km after leaving the track, you will cross a small wooden footbridge and then, a while later, the path descends some steps before you arrive at another large track, with the bridge of Puente de los Franceses to your left.

- Head down the track to the right (not over the bridge) and, after approximately 500 metres, drop down *(10)* to the left onto one of the paths you can see though the trees. You will continue to see white/yellow stripes. Follow that marked path until you see a sign to La Charca Verde *(11)*, a popular natural pool in the Manzanares river. (Swimming is forbidden. Wildlife is abundant here, and don't be surprised if you are approached by a group of ibex.)

- From La Charca Verde, return to the marked path and you will shortly come to a large track. Actually, there are a number of zigzags in the track here, which can be confusing. The best advice is to make your way to the river and cross it using one of the many footbridges, then swing right, following the path that runs southward along the eastern side of the river. Some paths lead off to the left, but stay as close to the river as possible. After a couple of kilometres, you will see some information boards, where you should cross the bridge *(12)* on your right. Follow the road around to the right and up the slope and you will find yourself in the Canto Cochino car park, with a couple of bars for refreshment.

- From the main Canto Cochino car park, head south on a large path that runs between the road (on your right) and the Manzanares river (on your left). After 600 metres, stay on the path as it veers to the right.

- You will shortly come to the road. Cross it and you will see a sign with a yellow arrow indicating the path on the other side. Follow that path as it runs parallel to the road, then gradually climbs and cuts across it a couple of times as it zigzags up the hill. You will also see occasional wooden signs for 'Senda' (path) on the way as the path (actually, a number of confluent paths) continues up the hill until you eventually arrive at the small car park of Quebrantaherraduras *(13)* on the col.

- Behind a sign for El Berzosillo/Canto Cochino, you will see white/yellow stripes painted on the rocks beyond; follow that well-marked path westwards. After 900 metres, the path takes a sharp right-hand bend, descends slightly, and then swings left again. When it has done so, turn left onto a smaller path *(14)* – there's a white/yellow cross on a rock at the turning. The path follows the course of a riverbed (which is often dry) towards the trees below. Just beyond the trees is a large dirt track. Turn left onto the track and follow it as it winds its way down the hill. After approximately 1 km, on a left-hand bend, there's a track to the right; a few metres beyond that, take a path to the right through the trees. You will shortly pass through a gate. Head down what is now a dirt track, between two walls, and then turn right onto a path leading upwards through an open field (ignore a path heading off to the left). Continue up that path alongside the wall to the top of the hill. You will now see the Ermita below. As you pass through a fallen wall, take a path left and then another right, in the direction of the Ermita. Now descend the hill, pass through a makeshift gate and you will soon be back at the Ermita car park.

APPROXIMATE GPS REFERENCES (UTM)

1	Ermita de San Isidro	422376 4509172
2	Clavijas	422726 4509863
3	Collado de Valdehalcones	422631 4510456
4	Ignore path to the left	422179 4510905
5	Shelter	420483 4512027
6	Collado Porrón	420258 4512244
7	Turn right to Maliciosa Baja	419416 4513092
8	Collado de los Pastores	420602 4513454
9	Turn right onto PR-M18	419874 4513498
10	Turn off track left	423309 4513404
11	La Charca Verde	423588 4512961
12	Bridge to Canto Cochino	424494 4511402

13	Quebrantaherraduras	424261 4510115
14	Turn left	423766 4510246

FOOTNOTE: THE CLAVIJAS

The short ascent on the Cuerda de Cabras is on a series of metal rods attached to the rock. It is a sort of mini via ferrata but without a cable. The rods are to stand on and to hold on to, but there is no means of tying on.

Peñalara in the snow - **WALK 20**

WALK NO. 20

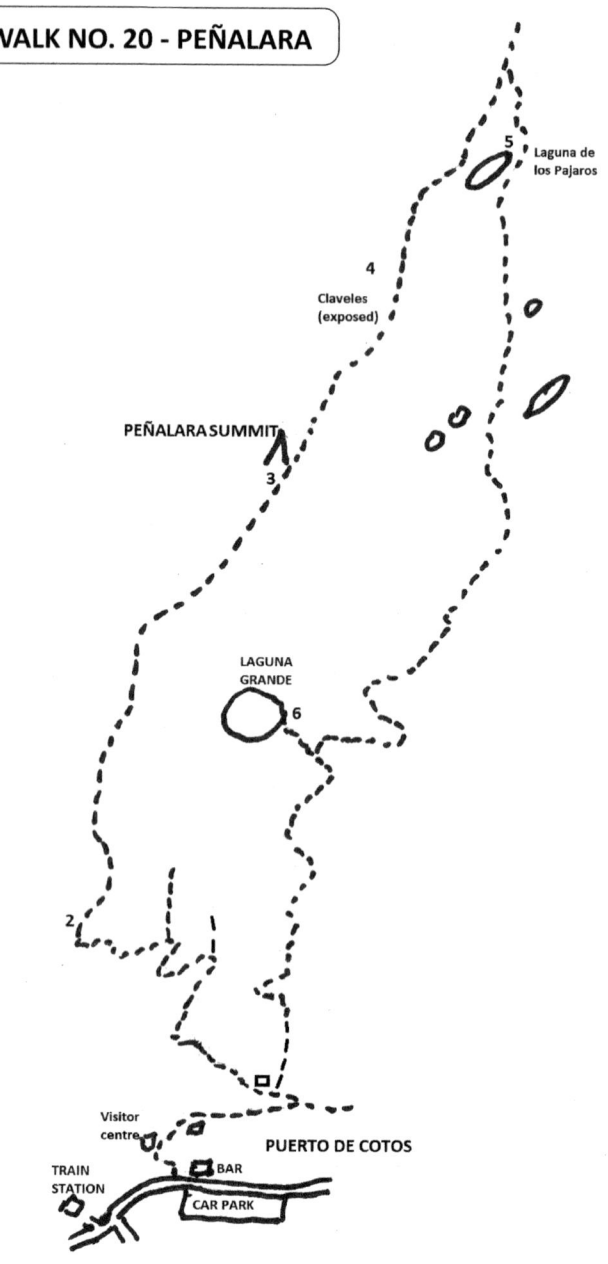

WALK NO. 20

PEÑALARA AND THE CINCO LAGUNAS

Distance	15 km
Ascent	860 metres
Overall grade	Strenuous
Terrain	Footpaths, good tracks, and a scramble on an exposed ridge
Exposure	Head for heights needed
Highest point	2,428 metres

A walk to the highest point in the Sierra Guadarrama National Park. A very easy ascent to the summit is followed by a scramble along a ridge, and then some easy footpaths to complete the circuit. It is graded as strenuous due to the difficulties posed by the scramble. In winter this walk should not be attempted without winter skills and equipment.

As an easy alternative, the peak of Peñalara can be reached by a simple out and back walk with no scrambling or exposure.

Being near Madrid, large numbers of people can arrive at weekends and bank holidays, to see the lagunas (tarns) which you will visit during the latter part of this walk. But the more difficult ridge is relatively quiet. To protect the environment, in this area it is not permitted to leave the established footpaths, so please respect this.

- The walk begins at the Puerto de Cotos *(1)*, on the M604, which links the Puerto de Navacerrada with the town of Rascafria. There is a large car park on the south side of the road. Cross the road and to the left of a bar/restaurant go up some steps and up a paved track to reach the second of two buildings, which is a visitor centre. To the right of it, and just beyond it, you will find a small round building (a security office) with a thatched roof.

- Walk up a broad track going north-east past the security office. After half a kilometre, you will reach a viewpoint with a movable arrow to show the names of the peaks in view. (The squeaky arrow could use a drop of oil!) At this point follow the track round a left-hand bend (do not take the track going straight on). You will find a building on the right, where a footpath turns right to go to the lagunas. Ignore it and stay on the main track. After another half-kilometre, you will reach a left-hand bend with a track going straight ahead. Take the left-hand bend. A further 200 metres along the track, a path goes to the right signposted to the Zabala refuge. Ignore it and stay on the main track.

- Keep going on the track as it zig-zags easily uphill. There are short cuts, but the authorities are prohibiting their use so as to regenerate eroded land. The track leads you to the first of two hill-tops, Hermana Menor (Little Sister) *(2)*, where you have a view to the north from the ridge line. Turn right along the broad ridge to reach the second hill top, Heremana Mayor (Big Sister). From here it is little more than an easy stroll for 1.25 kilometres to reach the summit of Peñalara *(3)*.

- For a peak as high as 2,429 metres (just over 8,000 feet) this must be the easiest one I have ever reached! If you want an easy summit (and the highest point in the Guadarrama Mountains) but do not want more of an adventure, it is worth coming this far and going back the same way. But for those who do the circuit, the easy part is over.

- From the summit, along the ridge line to the north-east you will see a sharp peak ahead, called the Risco de Claveles (2,387 metres) *(4)*. Our route goes over the top of it. It is tricky going on boulders, but in fact not quite as scary as it first appears. There are vertical drops to the east side, but there is no real need to go along that edge. However, there does not appear to be one correct route. I have seen strong walkers striding over the very summit without breaking their stride, whilst ordinary mortals find a way through the boulders. I personally took a line on what looked like a path on the east side, but found that I had to return to the top of the ridge to make progress. So, if you go along here, take care, and you will need to find the route that suits you best. It will not be suitable for vertigo sufferers. Although there is no great technical difficulty, it is airy. In winter conditions it is dangerous and should not be attempted without winter equipment and winter skills.

- So, scramble your way to the far end of the Risco de Claveles, where you will have a view below to the Laguna de los Pajaros. The route continues along the ridge line, now much easier, and a good path goes between two rocky summits, the Riscos de Pajaros, before starting a descent to the laguna.

- A former path goes straight down to the laguna, but it has been blocked, and you are now obliged by law to keep to the marked path, which takes you down to a point on the northern tip of the laguna *(5)*. Swimming is prohibited, for protection of dwindling wildlife. Many rare amphibians breed here and are under threat.

- From the southern side of the laguna a good path, marked at times with cairns and blue plaques (with a barely intelligible numbering system), goes to the south. Take this path, with the Riscos above on your right making a great view. You will pass through a level area called Cinco Lagunas (Five Lakes) although in the autumn some can be dry. The path descends, and crosses a stream on a wooden bridge before ascending once more to a point where you will see the Zabala refuge on the top of a rocky area to your right, and the large Laguna Grande below it. It would be easy to do an off-piste traverse to the laguna, but it is banned, so keep to the path which descends to cross the outlet stream on a bridge. From here our route goes left, but you can make a diversion to ascend slightly to the laguna, which you can circuit entirely before descending again to the bridge you just crossed.

- From there, a very easy footpath takes you, more or less on the same contour, all the way back to the building by the viewpoint you passed 0.5 kilometres from the start of the walk. Turn left and follow the track back to Cotos and the car park.

APPROXIMATE GPS REFERENCES (UTM)

1	Start and finish	419420 4522574
2	Hermana Menor	418608 4520947
3	Peñalara	419420 4522574
4	Risco de Claveles	419714 4523111
5	First laguna	420209 4523757
6	Laguna Grande	419325 4521402

WALK NO. 21

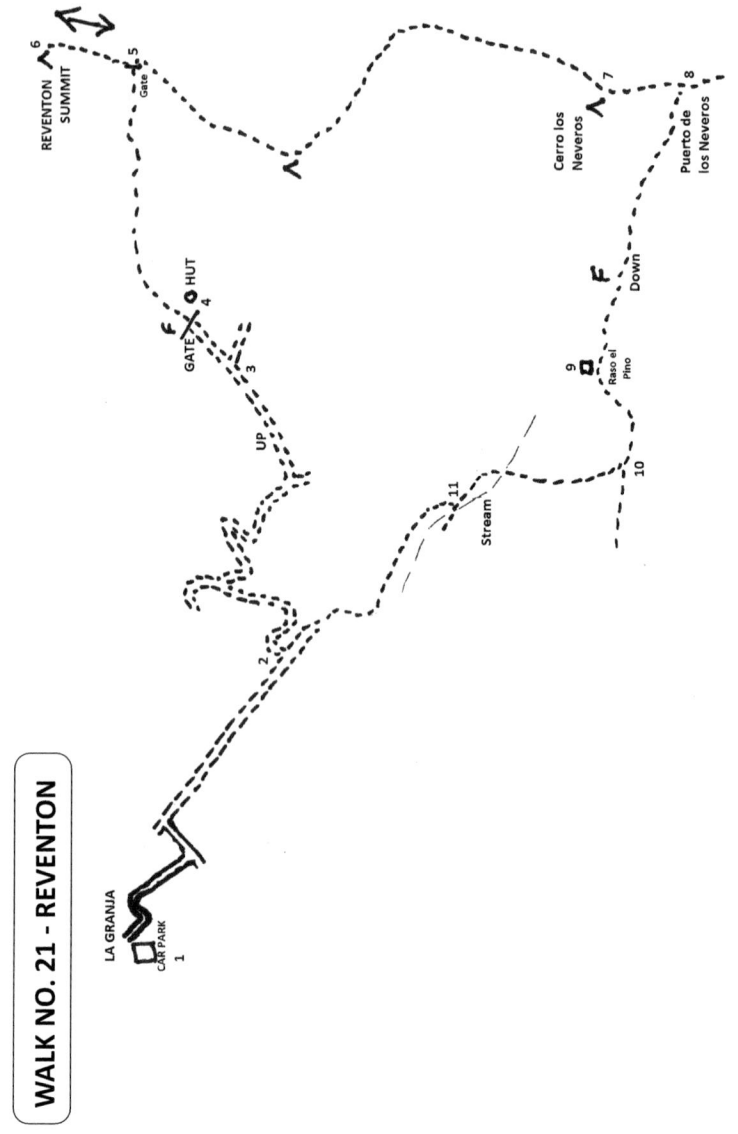

WALK NO. 21

REVENTON

Distance	24 km
Ascent	1,270 metres
Overall grade	Strenuous
Terrain	Good tracks and footpaths, with no difficulty underfoot
Exposure	None
Highest point	2,134 metres

A circular walk from the town of La Granja de San Ildefonso (Segovia) to the summit of Reventon, then along the high, broad ridge to the north of Peñalara, returning to the town via the pass Puerto de los Neveros.

The walk starts and ends in the delightful town of La Granja, to the north side of the Sierra de Guadarrama, and in the province of Segovia. The town is a cultural centre, being a monument to Spanish 18th century monarchy. It is home to a royal palace with gardens in the Versailles style. Details are on the Internet, but this is a guide to walking in the mountains, so we start in the town and just head for the hills.

- Driving from Segovia to La Granja on the CL601, as you enter the town centre there is a roundabout and to its left a large car park. Start the walk here *(1)*. Across the road to the south-east, a gateway leads to a street (Calle de la Alameda) which leads directly uphill through the centre. Continue up the street until you can go no further and then go left, before turning right to walk alongside the perimeter wall of the palace gardens, a typical estate wall. Go along, heading south-east alongside the wall for about 1.25 kilometres, and then go left on a broad track *(2)*. The track ascends in zigzags, and is occasionally marked with blue signs. Continue ascending on this track. Ignore any minor tracks. After about 3.5 kilometres on the track, keep left at a junction *(3)*. Continue until after a further 0.5 kilometres you reach a gate, beyond which is a *fuente*, and to the right of it a delightful old *chozo* (a shepherd's hut) *(4)*. The track continues to the left side of the wall.

- The track soon becomes a very nice footpath, crosses a stream, and swings right to follow a wall on the right up towards a col, the Puerto del Reventon *(5)*. At the col you will see a gate ahead, but do not go through it yet. Instead, turn left and make a very easy ascent to the rocky summit of Reventon, at 2,073 metres altitude *(6)*. From the trig point, return to the col, and now go through the gate. Then continue to the south-west along the broad ridge.

- Follow a path along the top of the ridge, firstly going south-west until reaching a top about 1.3 kilometres from the gate at 2,133 metres altitude. The path now veers to the south-east. After a little more than a further kilometre, the path leads round the head of a valley which is below to the right. Stay on high ground around the head of the valley. The path becomes indistinct, passing through heather undergrowth, but keep high and you will be on the right track. The path becomes clear again and the ridge will now lead you to the south until you reach a rocky summit at Cerro de los Neveros *(7)* (2,134 metres). The path skirts round the left-hand side of the rocks and then descends to the pass Puerto de los Neveros *(8)* at 2,096 metres. There is a crossroads of paths here. Straight ahead would lead you on to the major summit of Peñalara, but instead turn right on a footpath, with a stream valley below on your left.

- Follow this path downhill, heading north-west. At one point, a small sign shows the way to a *fuente*, which is shortly below the path on the right. Continue down the main path until you reach Raso el Pino *(9)*, a meadow with a meteorological station. Keep to the left of this and go straight on, on a track. It swings to the right and at a fork in the path keep right *(10)* and follow a very nice but very steep path with a stream below on the right.

- Continue straight down. The track crosses a bridge over a stream, and then after a further 300 metres, a stream goes underneath the track. Immediately before this, a footpath goes off to the right *(11)*. Take this path. It goes uphill but this is only temporary. Continue on this path. You may have to cross one or two fallen tree trunks, but otherwise there is no great difficulty. The stream is below to your left, and eventually the stream swings further left, with the path keeping to the right. Soon you will have good views down to the palace of La Granja, the path will lead you down to the top end of the estate wall, which you were following at the start of the walk. Follow the wall downhill and back into town.

APPROXIMATE GPS REFERENCES (UTM)

1	Start and finish (car park)	415085 4528361
2	Go left	416542 4527475
3	Keep left	418463 4527837
4	Fuente and Chozo	418801 4528147
5	Puerto del Reventon	420435 4528498
6	Reventon	420548 4528937
7	Cerro de los Neveros	420177 4525125
8	Puerto de los Neveros	420183 4524581
9	Raso el Pino	418347 4525199
10	Keep right	417799 4525043
11	Path to the right	417580 4526146

WALK NO. 22 - LA BOLA DEL MUNDO AND THE WESTERN CUERDA LARGA

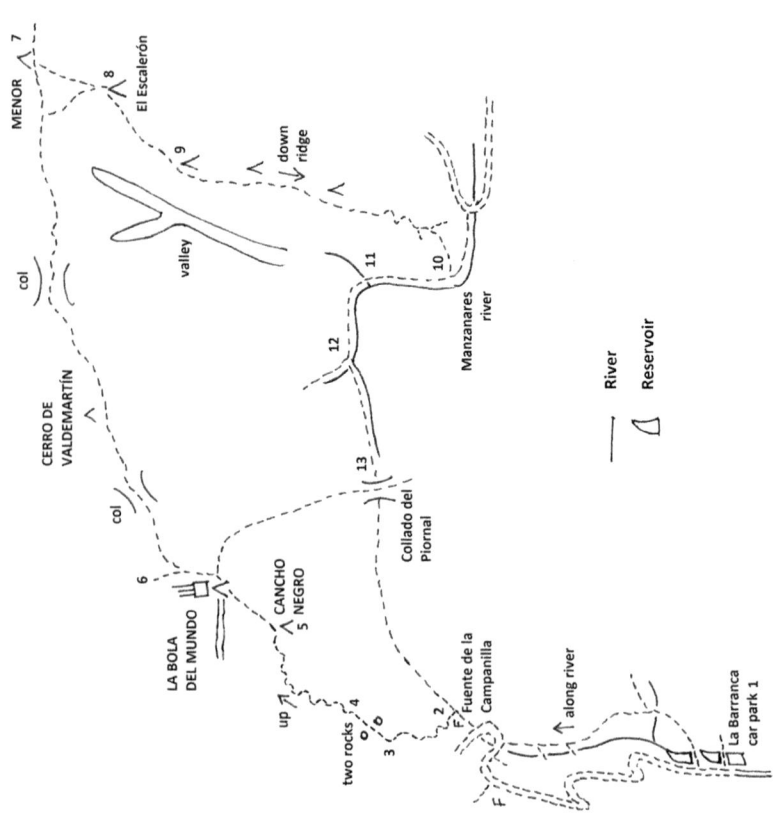

WALK NO. 22

LA BOLA DEL MUNDO AND THE WESTERN CUERDA LARGA

Distance	24 kilometres (or 12 kilometres for the shortened version)
Ascent	1500 metres (or 900 metres)
Overall grade	Very strenuous (or strenuous)
Terrain	Track, footpaths, loose rock and scrubland
Exposure	None, but some head for heights needed
Highest point	Cabeza de Hierro Menor: 2,374 metres

A long and demanding walk that climbs La Bola del Mundo (also known as Alto de las Guarramillas), via an unconventional route up its steep south side. It then climbs the western section of the Cuerda Larga to one of the highest peaks of the entire Guadarrama range, Cabeza de Hierro Menor, before returning by the little-used Loma de Cabezas and then along the Manzanares river. The overall altitude gain is considerable and there are sections that are slow going, so you should give yourself ample time to complete it. There is, however, an option for making the walk much shorter.

- The starting point is the car park of La Barranca *(1)*. The directions to get there are the same as for Walk 17.

- From the car park, walk up the main track. Ignore a gate to the first reservoir on the right. Continue past the barrier on the broad track and after 150 metres, pass through a gate on the right (it has a 'No Swimming' sign on it). Pass a small building with a sign 'Casa de Guias de Navacerrada' and cross the walkway over the reservoir.

- As you pass through the gate at the far end of the walkway, you will see a path heading straight ahead through the forest. Stay on that path (it actually forks at one point but the resulting two paths converge again) for approximately 500 metres as it swings left and drop down to a stream.

- Cross the stream, climb the bank and head along the path straight, ignoring a path ascending to the right. You will be heading in a northerly direction, parallel to the river on your left, which rises to your level as you ascend gradually through the forest. Ignore any paths to your left that tempt you to cross the river.

- After about 2 km of running parallel to the river, the path will eventually reach a large track. Swing left onto the track and then immediately right onto a path marked with white/yellow painted stripes. You will soon reach a crossing with another bend in the same track as before, marked with a stone obelisk and signpost.

- Cross the track following the arrow to Collado del Piornal/La Maliciosa and you will soon arrive at Fuente de la Campanilla (with the bell after which it is named). Immediately beyond the *fuente*, swing left and cross the stream at the easiest point you can see, then look for a path ascending through the trees *(2)*, marked with some small cairns. To begin with, the path is good, but quickly turns to loose rock as it starts to climb steeply. The path here is also less clear, but cairns and occasional faded white/green painted stripes mark the way.

- After about 1 km of ascent, you arrive at a large rock platform *(3)* on your left, an excellent viewpoint. Here the cairns seem to disappear. Head around the rocks to the right and you will find yourself in a large clearing, with two large rocks in the middle and the large peak of Cancho Negro behind them to the north-east – that's where you're heading. Head directly between the two rocks in the middle of the clearing (the left rock has a white/green marking on it) in a straight line in the direction of Cancho Negro and what looks like a gap in the trees ahead. (Ignore a cairn in the treeline in the lower part of the clearing to the left as that marks a different path.)

- As you approach the trees on the far side of the clearing, you'll start to see some cairns *(4)*, which are increasingly evident when you enter the trees and start to climb. The path, with significant loose rock in places, zigzags steeply upwards through the trees. The path can be slightly sketchy at times so make sure to follow the cairns. Once you emerge from the trees you will see jagged rocks above you, and the occasional view of the top of the chair lift across the valley to the north.

- Continue following cairns (and occasional white/green stripes that appear out of nowhere) as the path continues its steep ascent, skirting to the left of the jagged rocks (which offer some interesting scrambling if you wish). As you wind up and through the rocks you will ultimately, and quite suddenly, emerge on top of the peak of Cancho Negro *(5)*. Five hundred metres separate you from the radio masts on the higher, rounded summit of La Bola del Mundo. Make your way there in a straight line (the cairns can be hard to find among the mountain scrubland).

- From the geodesic marker at the summit, and facing the radio transmitters, make your way around them to the right.

- *(From here, it's possible to shorten the walk considerably. To do so, head downhill on the broad path on the right (east, ultimately veering south-east) marked with white/yellow stripes. This path will take you directly to Collado del Piornal (13), the col separating La Bola del*

Mundo and La Maliciosa. From there, turn right onto the marked path and continue to follow the directions from *** below).

- For the longer walk, continue around to the right of the radio transmitters and find another large path, next to some metal poles, heading north towards the rounded dome of Cerro de Valdemartín. Very shortly, and just as the path starts to descend, you will come to a fork. The correct path is the right-hand fork, but it is worth visiting a metal cone and tripod structure *(6)* about 100 metres down the left fork, which offers a 360-degree engraving depicting the surrounding peaks. Return to the right-hand fork and make your way down the hill on a clear, and at times rocky, path marked with white/yellow stripes (this is the PR-M11 path that runs the length of the Cuerda Larga).

- The path will take you to the col of Collado de las Guarramillas and then up the other side, alongside the fence on your left, to the top of Cerro de Valdemartín (the top of the ski lift is on your left and a small hut and mast on your right). From the top, continue on the same PR-M11 path down the other side until you arrive at the next col, Collado de Valdemartín, and then make the excellent and steeper ascent to Cabeza de Hierro Menor *(7)*, the 4th highest peak in the Guadarrama range and a splendid vantage point for views over the different valleys to the north, south and east. As you ascend, take note of a ridge of rocky outcrops (the Loma de Cabezas) that gradually descends into the valley to your right; that is where you will be descending later.

- From the summit of Cabeza de Hierro Menor, you have to make your way to El Escalerón, the first large rocky outcrop on Loma de Cabezas, the ridge stretching out to the south-west. You can do so directly, but the going is very rocky; the easiest route is to return approximately 400 metres down the path to the summit of Cabeza de

Hierro Menor, then swing left when you can see that you have a reasonably unimpeded route to El Escalerón. There's no actual path for either of the two options, but it's clear to see where you're heading. Once you have reached the top of El Escalerón *(8)*, drop back down to the right (north side) of it and start making your way down along the ridge. There is no path at this stage, but there are some very intermittent cairns and faded red dots to follow; my advice is to stay as close as possible to the right of the rocky outcrops as that's where the cairns and red dots are. However, this section can prove slow going as you scramble over and around rocks and through scrubland. Continue gradually down along the right of the ridge for approximately 800 metres from El Escalerón, making sure you keep a look out for cairns and red dots on the rocks as you go. You will suddenly see a cairn *(9)* on one of the rocks above you to the left. Make your way over to it and from here follow the cairns, which are far more frequent and easier to follow. You will soon also pass a rock arch, which can offer shelter if needed.

- Follow the cairns for a further 2.5 km down the ridge as it leads you down to the valley floor to the south. However, after you have passed the last hump of the ridge, and as you approach the valley floor, the cairns suddenly disappear; more accurately, as you look you'll find that random cairns seem to be dotted around with no rhyme or reason. However, you are heading for the river (the Manzanares river, which you might be able to hear) running west to east at the bottom of the valley in front of you. It is about 400 metres away. Make your way there following the path of least resistance; my advice is to swing gradually right as you go. Next to the river is a clear path *(10)* marked with cairns and white/yellow stripes. Turn right onto the path and follow it as it runs parallel to the river (which is to your left) up the valley.

- After a while, stay on the path as it crosses a tributary *(11)* of the Manzanares river and continue parallel to the main watercourse as it bends around 90 degrees left. After approximately 700 metres of further climbing alongside the river, you will see a shallow gully on the other side, rising to your left (west). Cross the river *(12)* at the easiest point you can find and start heading up the gully; there's a path on the right-hand side of it, which proves much easier going. After 1 km, you will arrive at Collado del Piornal *(13)*, with its rain gauge – a small metal tripod-like structure, marked on maps as *pluviómetro*.

- *** This is where the shorter walk joins the longer one.

- At the Collado del Piornal continue straight over it onto a path that descends the gully, following the course of the river all the way back to Fuente de la Campanilla (about 2 km). As far as the *fuente*, this is the same path as is used in Walk 16. The path is slippery in places due to loose rock. (See my comments in Walk 16.) From the *fuente*, continue down what is now a broad path until you arrive at a large track with a sign and a stone obelisk. Continue straight on to the path on the other side and follow it a short distance until you meet the broad dirt track again. Turn right and follow the track 2 km back to the main car park.

APPROXIMATE GPS WAYPOINTS (UTM)

1	La Barranca car park	416170 4511756
2	Path behind Fuente	416429 4513779
3	Rock platform	416285 4514098
4	Path at end of clearing	416417 4514280
5	Cancho Negro	416979 4514739
6	Cone 360-degree map	417477 4515624
7	Cabeza de Hierro Menor	420866 4516552

LA BOLA DEL MUNDO AND THE WESTERN CUERDA LARGA

8	El Escalerón	420647 4516005
9	Cairn	420178 4515665
10	Path by Manzanares river	419418 4513625
11	Cross tributary	419377 4514230
12	Cross Manzanares river to head up gully	418805 4514405
13	Collado del Piornal	417963 4514134

Cuerda Larga - **WALK 22**

WALK NO. 23

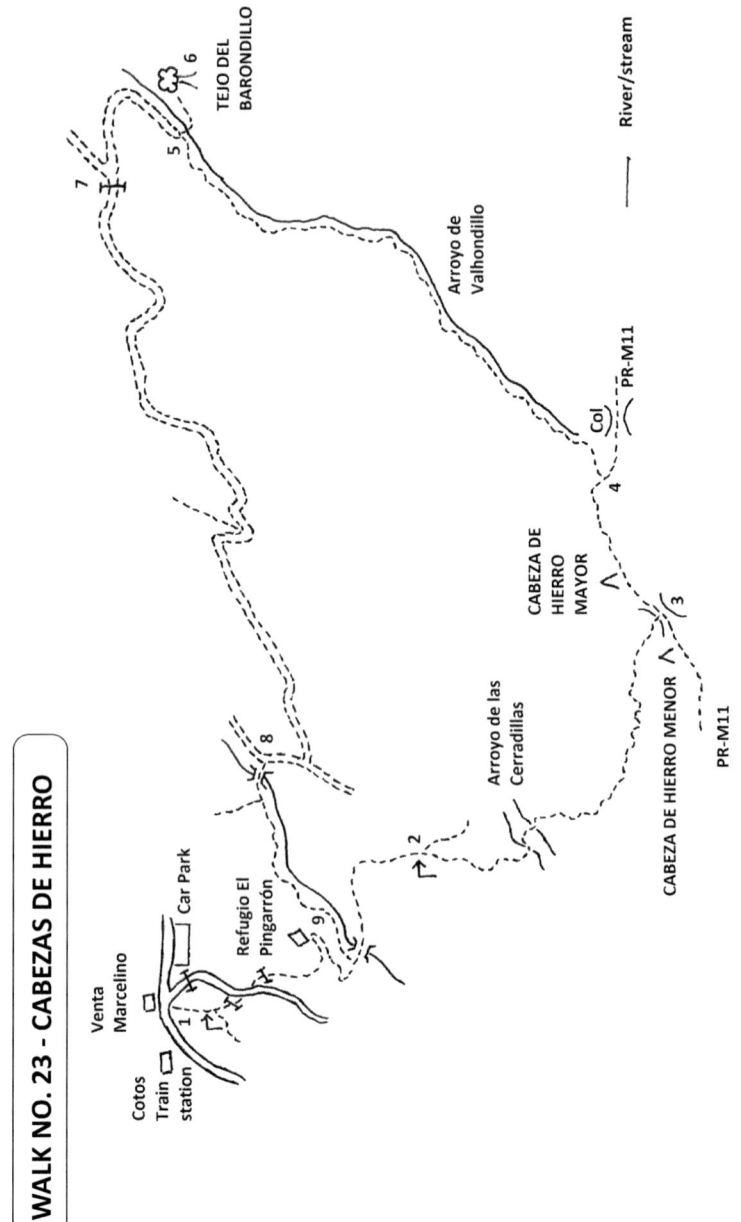

WALK NO. 23

CABEZAS DE HIERRO

Distance	23 km
Ascent	1,200 metres
Overall grade	Strenuous
Terrain	Footpaths, boulders and woodland tracks
Exposure	None
Highest point	Cabeza de Hierro Mayor: 2,381 metres

A walk that climbs the rocky Cabezas de Hierro (Menor and Mayor), two of the highest peaks in the entire Guadarrama range (the 3rd and 4th, respectively) and the highest points of the Cuerda Larga ridge, returning via a river valley and an ancient yew, one of the oldest trees in the Iberian Peninsula.

- The walk begins at the Puerto de Cotos, on the M604, which links the Puerto de Navacerrada with the town of Rascafria. There is a large car park on the south side of the road.

- By the car park, and next to the junction with the road to Valdesquí (often blocked by a barrier), take a wide path *(1)* next to a sign for Real Sitio de San Idelfonso/ Montes de Valsaín that climbs some stone steps. The path is marked with wooden posts indicating the RV1 and RV9 routes, and white/yellow stripes of the PR-M27 route. You will soon come to a wooden sign; follow the arrow to 'Ref. Pingarrón'. As you gradually descend, you will come to a barrier and a road; cross the road, pass another barrier and continue to follow the white/ yellow stripes and wooden RV1/RV9 marker posts along a track.

- As you take a left-hand bend, you will arrive at Refugio Juvenil El Pingarrón, which, despite its name, doesn't offer shelter and is frequently closed. Continue on the marked path as it takes a sharp right turn and starts to descend through the trees. After 500 metres or so, cross the wooden footbridge over the Arroyo de las Guarramillas river and continue on the marked path as it starts to climb again gradually through the woods. As you reach the top of the hump, you will see the two peaks of Cabezas de Hierro before you (the slightly taller and broader 'Mayor' on the left and the more pointed 'Menor' on the right). You immediately start to descend again and will eventually arrive at a fork and wooden sign *(2)*. Take the right fork following the arrow to 'Cabezas de Hierro – 2.8 km'. You will now no longer see the wooden marker posts, but will still see the white/yellow stripes of PR-M27.

- The path continues down through the trees and then crosses a series of streams/muddy riverbeds that are part of Arroyo de las Cerradillas, before ascending again. When you ultimately emerge from the trees, the path, still marked with white/yellow, starts to climb through scrubland towards the Cabezas de Hierro peaks. Cairns are more prevalent here and are often easier to follow than the stripes. The going becomes increasingly steep and rocky and you might have to use hands occasionally to scramble over boulders.

- After about 1 km since emerging from the treeline, the white/yellow stripes inexplicably stop; however, there are plenty of cairns to mark the way. As you look up, the peak above is Cabeza de Hierro Menor; its bigger sister is currently hidden behind the hump of the ridge on your left. Follow the cairns (there's no real path in places) that you can see on the left-hand side of the gully heading upward, which you can see starts to bend around to the left (east) above. (Ignore any cairns that try to take you directly in the direction of the rocky peak.) The cairned rocky path continues up the left-hand side of that gully and, as you start to come level with the top of the hump on the left, the cairns make a beeline for the col between the two Cabezas de Hierro peaks. Follow the cairns and sketchy path to the col *(3)*.

- Once at the col, you will find the larger, well-marked PR-M11 path running left to right joining the two peaks (the PR-M11 used to be marked with painted white/yellow stripes, but these have been replaced with white/yellow metal strips, which have since lost their colour; hence, you will be following grey metal strips). Swing right and climb to the summit of Cabeza de Hierro Menor for views over the west of the Guadarrama range; then return to the col and climb the path to the top of Cabeza de Hierro Mayor, the highest point on the Cuerda Larga, the long, broad ridge that you can now see, running eastward.

- From the summit, continue east along the PR-M11 (markings are sparse here but the path is clear), which descends to the Collado de Peña Vaqueros col. Just before the path levels out at the col, you will see a series of large cairns heading left (south-east) off the path, towards a gully, the Arroyo de Valhondillo. Turn off the path left *(4)* and follow the cairns cross-country downhill, to the start of the gully and a stream. Follow the watercourse down; at this early stage you can hop to either side, whichever is easier going, but you will eventually have to stay on the left side of the river. There are also no cairns here so just follow what is now a river as close as you comfortably can on its left bank. At times you will have to leave the river as it starts dropping down steeper along gullies and waterfalls. However, as soon as you can, venture back to it.

- You will eventually see intermittent cairns marking a way through the undergrowth (the path is more intuitive than anything else as it follows narrow cattle paths down alongside the river); if you lose them, just stay close to the river and they will appear again eventually. The valley ultimately broadens, and then bends around to the left; here the path is somewhat more evident. However, you will reach a clearing of sorts, with rocks up to your left, where the path disappears again. Continue in the same direction you were going along the river, finding the path of least resistance, and drop gradually to another clearing below. In the middle there are a couple of isolated cairns.

- The river bends right again here; continue to follow it and enter trees, where a path becomes increasingly evident as you go. The river drops significantly down to your right, and you'll therefore be unable to follow it as closely as before, although you should still hear it. Follow what is now a clearer path until it ultimately emerges onto the start of a large dirt track *(5)*. Rather than head down the track, find a cairn to the right and follow the path that drops to the river below. Cross the river over rocks at the easiest point you can find and then swing left along the opposite bank. After 100 or so metres, you will come to the Tejo del Barondillo *(6)* – an ancient yew that is reputed to be between 1,500 and 1,800 years' old, one of the oldest trees in the Iberian Peninsula – which is fenced to protect it from human encroachment.

- Return to the dirt track and head down it. After 1 km, where the track takes a sharp right-hand bend, ignore the bend and continue straight onto another track *(7)* past a metal barrier. Continue along this track for 4 km, with views to Peñalara to the north, until you come to a broken barrier. Ignore a path to the right and continue on the track for a further 1.5 km until you reach another dirt track crossing left to right. Swing right, past a marker post for the RV1 and RV9 routes, and follow the track for 250 metres until you come to another marker post, old wooden sign, and large path to your left *(8)*.

- Turn left onto the large path, cross the stone bridge over the river and then turn left at the next fork. You will be able to see the Pingarrón refuge above you through the gap in the trees. After a further 300 metres, the large path crosses the river (ignore a small path on the left of the river before you cross) and climbs sharply leaving the river below to your left. The climb is a case of 'two steps forward, one step back' at times as the path is mostly loose rock and earth.

- The path eventually levels out onto a good cairned path and the riverbed soon rises up from the rocks to your left to run alongside it. Continue along this wonderful path along the river as both gradually climb through the forest. There are plenty of natural pools along the way, even in summer. One particularly excellent spot for a rest is the Poza de Sócrates *(9)*, which includes a waterfall and rock pool. From the Poza, continue along the path some metres further and you will emerge next to the wooden bridge that you crossed earlier (to your left).

- From here, return via the outward route: i.e. turn right here up the clear path (marked with white/yellow stripes and posts indicating the RV 1 and 9 routes) and follow it 1.5 km back past the Pingarrón refuge, across the road and back to the Puerto de Cotos car park.

APPROXIMATE GPS WAYPOINTS (UTM)

1	Start of the marked path	418858 4519571
2	Signpost, turn right	419741 4518079
3	Col	421099 4516694
4	Turn left off PR-M11 path	421892 4517033
5	Start of large track	423878 4519410

6	Tejo de Barondillo	423982 4519368
7	Continue straight onto track	423667 4519831
8	Turn left	420316 4518992
9	Poza de Sócrates	419175 4518511

Bola del Mundo from Cabezas de Hierro - **WALK 23**

LA NAJARRA AND ASOMATE DE HOYOS FROM PUERTO DE LA MORCUERA

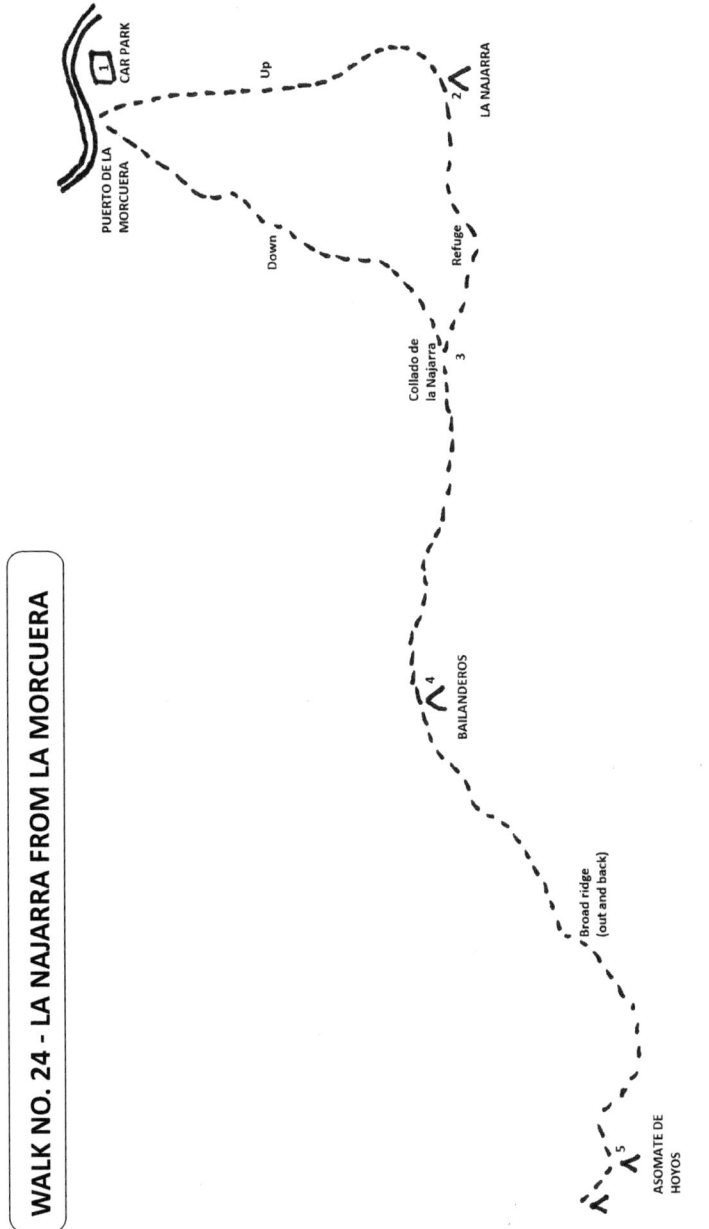

WALK NO. 24

LA NAJARRA AND ASOMATE DE HOYOS FROM PUERTO DE LA MORCUERA

Distance	14 km
Ascent	800 metres
Overall grade	Moderate
Terrain	Grass, some rocky areas and good footpaths
Exposure	None
Highest point	2,242 metres

An easy ascent to the eastern-most summits of the Cuerda Larga ridge. The route consists of an ascent to the peak of La Najarra, followed by a traverse to the summit of Asomate de Hoyes, returning partly by the same route but with a different descent from the ridge. *(See the footnotes for a general description of the full Cuerda Larga route.)*

- Puerto de la Morcuera is on the M611 road between Miraflores de la Sierra and Rascafria. Driving from Miraflores, continue on this road until the very top of the hill, just beyond kilometre 9. Park in a car park on the left just before the pass *(1)*.

- From the car park, walk up a stairway to the top of the pass and find a signpost showing that you are entering the El Paular valley. There is a strange structure which I believe to be a windbreak. Go through a gate here, and to the left there is a wire fence ascending the slope to the south. Follow the fence to begin with and then keep going south over open country of grass and heather, all the way to the summit of La Najarra (2,121 metres) *(2)*. There are cairns marking the route and you may find paint marks. It is an easy ascent of 360 metres height and 1.5 kilometres distance. Just over half way up the incline you will cross a minor rocky top. Otherwise there is little of note. However, the ascent is well worthwhile and the ridge provides great long-distance views in all directions.

- The summit is rocky with a trig point. From there, turn right and follow the top of the ridge to the west. Simply keep to the high ground. Further directions are not necessary. The broad ridge soon takes you to the old stone-built refuge Refugio de la Najarra. It is badly deteriorated, and only provides the minimum amount of shelter, but it is very picturesque.

- From the refuge, descend to the col Collado de la Najarra *(3)*, and then ascend on a good path to the west to reach the second summit Los Bailanderos (2,133 metres) *(4)*. This is a rocky top with a cairn marking the highest point.

- You can continue along the ridge for as far as you like, always remembering that if you want to return to your vehicle you will need to turn round at some point and retrace your steps as far as the Collado de la Najarra.

- Continuing farther on the ridge, the third main summit is Asomate de Hoyos (2,242 metres) *(5)*.

- Unless you wish to continue along the ridge, turn round at Asomate de Hoyos and walk back to Collado de la Najarra, which is just before starting the ascent to the Refugio de la Najarra. At the col *(3)*, take a footpath descending to the north-east. This is part of the PR-M11 path, marked with yellow and white paint. It descends gradually along the northern flanks of La Najarra and back to the start of the walk.

WALK NO. 24

APPROXIMATE GPS WAYPOINTS (UTM)

1	Start	429862 4520020
2	La Najarra summit	430172 4518607
3	Collado de la Najarra	428751 4518409
4	Los Bailanderos	427116 4518513
5	Asomate de Hoyos	425527 4517578

FOOTNOTES: CUERDA LARGA

We do not include the full ridge as a separate walk in this book, due to the logistical transport difficulties. The Cuerda Larga (the Long Chain) is a linear ridge with nine major summits, over a distance of approximately 22 kilometres. The western extreme is Puerto de Navacerrada, and the eastern is Puerto de la Morcuera. This walk, Walk 24, visits the eastern parts of the ridge, returning to Puerto de la Morcuera, and thereby removing the transport problems.

Cuerda Larga from La Pedriza

MIRAFLORES TO LA NAJARRA AND PICO PERDIGUERA

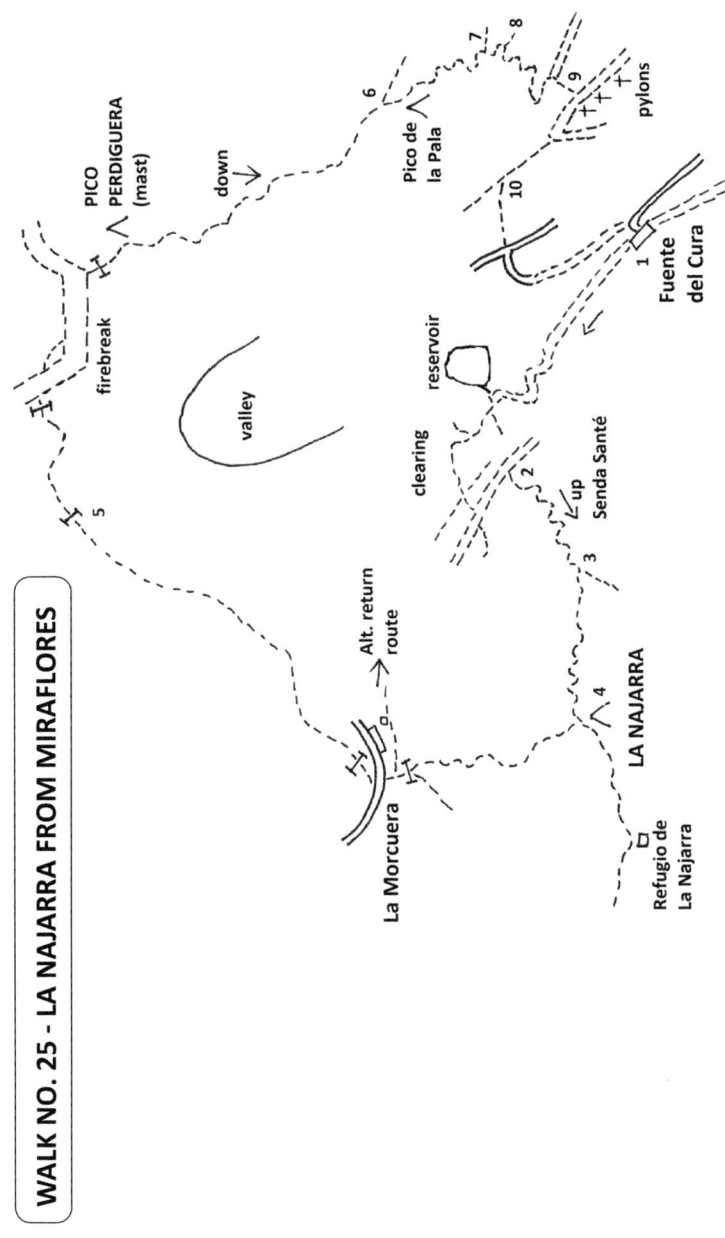

WALK NO. 25

MIRAFLORES TO LA NAJARRA AND PICO PERDIGUERA

Distance	26 km
Ascent	1350 metres
Overall grade	Strenuous
Terrain	Tracks and footpaths
Exposure	None
Highest point	La Najarra: 2,120 metres

La Najarra is the first destination in Walk 24, when approached from the north. This walk, Walk 25, goes to the same peak from the south-east. It is at the eastern end of the Cuerda Larga, well worth a visit if just for its 360 views over La Pedriza to the west, Peñalara and Montes Carpetanos to the north, the Sierra Norte to the east and the Madrid plateau to the south. This walk takes a longer and steeper route to the peak from the village of Miraflores and returns via the long ridge that descends from Pico Perdiguera.

- The walk starts at the Fuente del Cura car park *(1)*, in the village of Miraflores de la Sierra. As you arrive at the village, you will start to see signs towards 'Area Recreativa Fuente del Cura'. Follow them through the village until you cross a small bridge into the Fuente del Cura car park. There is a long and narrow car park on the right and the fountain of Fuente de la Villa on the left.

- As you face the Fuente de la Villa fountain, head right (north-west) to the end of the tarmacked car park. At the end there is an information board for Puerto de La Morcuera. Immediately beyond the sign there is a track, which you follow to the left. You will start to see painted white/yellow and white/green stripes, or a combination of both, on lampposts and trees.

- Continue up the track as it slowly ascends (ignoring an open gate on the right) until you reach a barrier across the track. Continue past the barrier and ignore the turnstile to the dam and Miraflores reservoir on your right, instead swinging left onto the wide path, still following the white/yellow/green marks.

- After crossing a cattle grid, ignore the path to the left just beyond it, and continue straight on. From here the best thing is to follow the white/green stripes on rocks, trees and, occasionally, poles; they are quite evident. Ignore any paths to the right, and the marked path will emerge from the trees, crossing a stream, ascending out into an open clearing. The marked path heads up towards the treeline and meets a path, crossing left to right, that runs parallel to the treeline.

- Continue straight ahead across the path and into the trees, still following the white/green stripes. You will soon arrive at a larger track above. Here you swing left, leaving the white/green marks. After approximately 500 metres, you will see a large cairn on the right of the track (and another on the left, which you ignore), which marks the beginning of a path known as the Senda Santé. Turn right onto the Senda Santé *(2)*, which zigzags up the steep slope for about 1 km before finally emerging from the trees. The terrain of the path then changes to loose rock, still in a steep ascent. The path, now in the open, continues to zigzag upwards around rocky outcrops to what turns out to be a false summit.

- Just as you think you have reached the peak, the path levels out onto a plateau and rocks, where you will find a large cairn marking what is known as Cuatro Calles (Four Streets) *(3)*; from here you will see that the La Najarra peak is still some way away, above you to the north-west. Cairns continue to mark the path across a flatter section of open grassland in the direction of the peak. It then becomes rocky again as it ascends.

- After about 2 km of ascent from Cuatro Calles, you will finally reach the La Najarra peak *(4)* (the geodesic marker is the official peak, but is slightly lower than the actual peak: the rocky outcrops some 100 metres to the east). From the official peak you will see a number of metal poles that once used to be a fence running in a northerly direction down the hill, and a path next to them.

- From the peak start descending the path to the north, along the line of fence posts. The path takes you on a descent which is rocky at times, with a short scramble, although with no exposure. There are occasional white/green marks and grey painted stripes where those markings have been painted over. The path is reasonably evident, but the further you descend, it gets sketchier in places. If in doubt, a fence will guide you on the path of least resistance to the road and car park of La Morcuera, which you can see below you. Pass through a metal gate to reach the road.

- *(From here, it is possible to shorten the walk considerably. If you wish to do so, swing right along the wooden fence, following the sign to Fuente del Cura. You will descend some steps, past an information hut. Continue down onto a track towards a wooden stile. As soon as you have passed through, descend left onto a path below and then swing right. Continue on that path as it hugs the treeline for 2.5 km until you see the white/green stripes you were following earlier. As soon as you do, turn left, and follow them back to the starting point.)*

- For the longer walk, cross the road and head for a large wooden sign to your left reading Rascafría/Puerto Morcuera 1,796m. Walk up the track behind the sign. It soon turns into a path and passes through a makeshift wire gate in a fence. The clear path continues through the trees and you will start to see cairns. After about 1km, you will see a fence on your left, to which the path runs parallel for a further 2km.

- As you arrive at a col (you will see that a gully starts to drop away to the right) and small clearing, the path disappears. Look to the fence on the left and you will see a gate *(5)* made of wire and logs; pass through the gate and follow the path on the other side as it swings right, running parallel to the fence. The path now widens out as it ascends, then bends right towards the treeline, still along the fence, and then left again. Approximately 1 km after the previous gate, pass through another similar gate and turn right onto a large firebreak.

- Stay on the firebreak as it bends left (a cairn on your left marks a small shortcut if you want to take it) and continue, with fences on both sides at one stage, until you reach yet another gate. Pass through and turn right onto the path that heads towards the mast on Pico Perdiguera, the highest peak on the Cuerda de las Vaqueriza ridge, which offers views to the eastern end of the range.

- On the far side of the mast, cairns mark a path that descends the broad Cuerda de las Vaqueriza ridge you can see below to the south. The path, with a lot of loose rock in places, meanders around the rocky outcrops and secondary peaks along the ridge.

- After about 3 km of descent from the mast, the loose rock disappears for a while and a wire fence appears on your left. Soon after, you will see a cluster of cairns *(6)* in the path; these mark a fork. It's important to take the right fork towards the Pico de la Pala (despite the name, not really much of peak, rather a rocky outcrop 50 metres beyond the cairns). Continue over the top and you will see cairns marking a path that descends the other side. Follow it and you will also start to see some white/green paint markings (although these are very intermittent).

- Stay on that descending path, which will start to zigzag quite significantly through the trees. Ignore any paths to the left, including one with cairns *(7)*. A little further down, also on the left there's a viewpoint (painted on a rock as 'Mirador') *(8)*. However, continue to descend on the same path you were on, still ignoring any tangents to the left. You will cross a fallen rock wall and then a small bridge as the path zigzags through the forest.

- Eventually, after a sharp left-hand bend, the path starts to run alongside a wall, then re-enters the trees and bends right along the wall. Here you will suddenly find a metal pole marking the white/green SL01 route, with an arrow pointing back where you have just come from. Ignore the pole, arrow and the large track to the left; continue straight on to the track you can see some metres further ahead, with power pylons running along it left to right *(9)*.

- When you reach that track with the pylons, turn right, following it past a building on the right. When the track bends sharply left, continue straight onto the wide path ahead (a small path then forks along the wall to the left – ignore that). That wide path, with occasional white/green stripes, runs between two walls; after 800 metres, just before emerging from the trees, take a path to the left *(10)* (there's a white/green cross on a rock next to it).

- After a short descent, you reach a road. Cross the road and take a road on the other side, signposted: Albergue, El Colladito, Multiaventura. Stay on that road for a short while until you reach a large signpost for 'El Colladito and Alta Ruta de Guadarrama', where you turn left.

- As you follow that road, tarmac soon changes to dirt track. You will pass a number of properties, and after approximately 500 metres on your right, you will see the bridge into the Fuente del Cura car park.

APPROXIMATE GPS WAYPOINTS (UTM)

1	Fuente de la Villa fountain	433916 4518387
2	Turn right onto Senda Santé	432051 4519026
3	Cuatro Calles	431284 4518520
4	La Najarra peak	430162 4518596
5	Pass through gate in fence	431857 4522179
6	Turn right at cairn cluster	434746 4519786
7	Ignore cairns to left	435020 4518933
8	Mirador	434856 4518765
9	Turn right following pylons	434786 4518524
10	Turn left off large path, rock with X	434185 4518966

El Yelmo summit

WALK NO. 26 - LA PEDRIZA AND EL YELMO

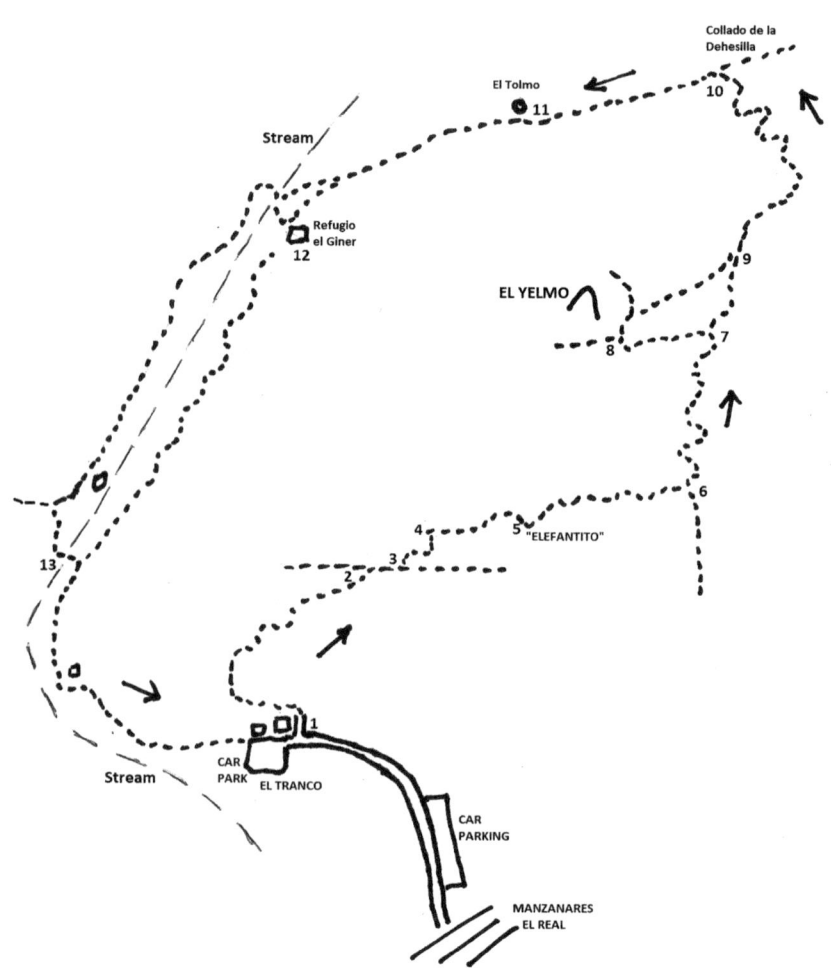

WALK NO. 26

LA PEDRIZA AND EL YELMO

Distance	17 km
Ascent	870 metres
Overall grade	Strenuous
Terrain	Steep, stony footpaths and boulders
Exposure	None, unless you climb to the summit
Highest point	1,605 metres

A beautiful walk into the granite national park of La Pedriza, visiting the remarkable elephant-shaped rock 'El Elefantito', and with an ascent to the base of El Yelmo, one of the most emblematic peaks of the area.

The summit of El Yelmo can only be reached as a rock climb, or by a difficult scramble up a narrow chimney on the north-eastern side of the peak. I do not include any further instructions on that, as it is really outside the scope of this book.

La Pedriza is a Natural Park within the National Park of the Sierra Guadarrama. Although there is a car park part way along this walk, vehicle access is restricted at peak times. However, you can walk into the Natural Park at any time by following the river Manzanares from El Tranco at Manzanares el Real. The area is a labyrinth of rocks and it is easy to get lost (I know from experience) so I am using plenty of GPS references to help you.

- From Madrid, take the M607 motorway north, go past Tres Cantos and Colmenar Viejo, turn right on to the M609, then left on to the M608. Shortly, a further left turn leads to the small town of Manzanares el Real. Go past the spectacular castle and at the far (western) end of town turn right at a roundabout and go back towards the town centre. Then the first turn to the left goes to the visitor centre of La Pedriza, but ignore that turn and instead take the second left into Avenida de la Pedriza. This avenue ascends through a smart housing area to reach a dead end with a small car park. If the car park is full there is more parking just back down the road. (It gets busy here at weekends and bank holidays.) There is a small roundabout just before the car park and to its right look for the bar/restaurant Casa Julian *(1)*.

- Walk into an alleyway which goes to the right-hand side of the bar/restaurant. At the end of the alley ascend over rocky ground. Turn left where yellow paint points towards El Yelmo. Follow the path in zigzags uphill, at first in a westerly direction, but soon turning to the north and then north-east. There is only one path here, so just stay on it. The path is known as the Senda de las Carboneras (the Coal Bunkers path). (It is an officially-numbered path, the RV-25.) The path twists and turns, so take care not to lose it. It is quite steep at times.

- After about 1.5 kilometres uphill walking, you will emerge on to a level, open meadow. At this point a path joins from the left and continues to the right across the meadow *(2)*. Take this path to the right, more or less on the level, and going east. It is one of the variants of the long-distance path GR 10, but you should follow it for only 300 metres, and then take a minor path uphill to the left *(3)*. As you go northwards on this path, look ahead and to the right and aim for a valley behind the first ridge. The path goes north for a few metres, and then swings to the north-east to ascend that valley *(4)*, where it zigzags gradually uphill.

- Along this path, and about 750 metres walking from where you left the GR10, you will find one of the highlights of La Pedriza, el Elefantito, or the 'Little

Elephant' *(5)*. (When you see it you will not need me to explain why it has that name!)

- Standing with your back to the elephant's trunk, go to the right and almost immediately left again on a path going east. It becomes a vaguer path farther on, but press on in a direction just north of east, and at times downhill. After just over half a kilometre, you will reach a route marked with yellow and white paint *(6)*. I refer to it as a route rather than as a path because much of it crosses bare rock. At this point turn left, uphill and keep a keen eye open to follow the paint marks. (This is another numbered route, the PR-M1.)

- At an altitude of 1,580 metres, where the terrain begins to level out, take a path to the left *(7)*. This will lead you quickly to the base of the dome of El Yelmo. Its summit is at 1,719 metres altitude. It is far from being one of the highest peaks, but it can be seen for miles and is one of the area's main landmarks. The meadows below the peak make a great place for a rest. It is common to see herds of *cabra montesa* (ibex) here.

- There are paths all over the place here. From the meadows before the peak *(8)* just head north-east, and find a path which leads you in that direction keeping a ridge above on your left. Continue in that direction until you rejoin the major, paint-marked path *(9)*. Go left, north, along this path, and as you go round the end of the hillside follow it down a rocky area as it descends to the col of La Dehesilla. You will need to pick your way down the rocks but they are not especially difficult. La Dehesilla *(10)* is a delightful mountain pass, where the main GR10 path crosses from east to west. It is marked with red and white markers.

- From the col, follow the red and white markers down the path going west into a valley. Continue until you reach a huge rock, El Tolmo *(11)* next to the path. Then continue on the paint-marked path to the south-west to reach the mountain refuge at El Giner *(12)*. It is open normally only at weekends to provide refreshments.

- From the refuge, follow the main well-walked path to the right and down to the river, cross a bridge, turn left and follow the right bank on a broad track known as the 'Autopista' (motorway). About 2 kilometres from the refuge, you will reach a fenced building on the left. Go past the gates and then keep left. Do not cross the bridge to the right, but go on to the next bridge on your left and then cross the stream *(13)*. Then turn immediately right to follow the left bank of the stream all the way back to El Tranco and the start of the walk.

- ***As an alternative from the refuge***, a more sporty and interesting path goes in a south-westerly direction, staying above the left bank of the stream. You will have to search for the path, or ask somebody at the refuge, but it is not far away. (You should be able to find it in the vicinity of GPS waypoint *(14)* below.) Once you are on it, the path divides and re-joins at times, and it is rough and stony. There is no correct or incorrect path, but the main thing is not to stray too far from the stream valley. If you find yourself making a significant ascent to the south, go back and find the river path. Eventually you will emerge on to open ground. Continue in the same direction, and keeping the river always on your right you will arrive at El Tranco, where you began the walk. This last section of 2 to 3 kilometres is an easy and popular path, but goes through beautiful country and makes a great finish to the walk.

APPROXIMATE GPS WAYPOINTS (UTM)

1	Start and finish	425458 4510508
2	Meadows and GR10 path	425785 4511261
3	Minor path left	426001 4511281

LA PEDRIZA AND EL YELMO

4	Path up the valley	426042 4511406
5	El Elefantito	426508 4511522
6	Yellow and white paint	427085 4511618
7	Turn left	427144 4512305
8	Meadows	426814 4512286
9	Rejoin paint-marked path	427317 4512682
10	Collado de la Dehesilla	427152 4513442
11	El Tolmo	425961 4513151
12	Giner refuge	425433 4512855
13	Stream crossing	424589 4511312
14	Alternative path	425334 4512741

La Pedriza - **WALK 26**

WALK NO. 27 - LAS TORRES

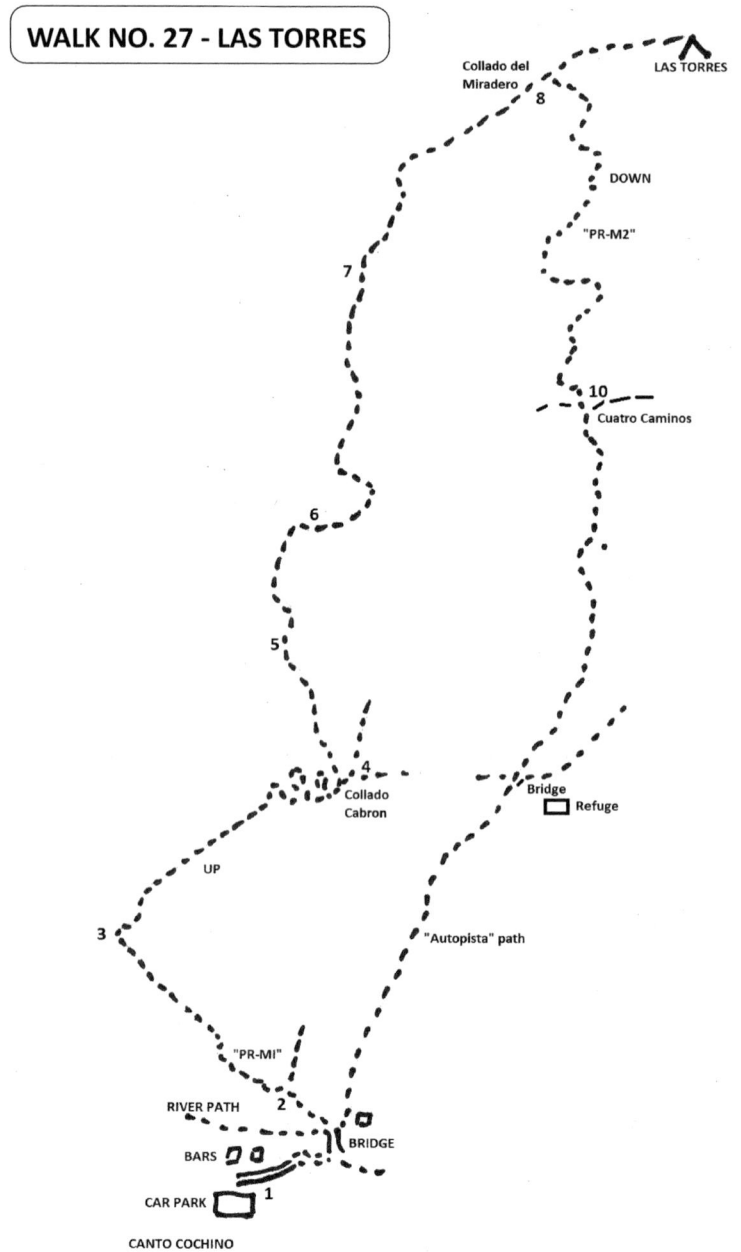

WALK NO. 27

LAS TORRES DE LA PEDRIZA

Distance	17 km
Ascent	1,200 metres
Overall grade	Strenuous
Terrain	Good footpaths, some difficult rocky scrambles, some broad tracks, and lots of twists and turns
Exposure	Moderate exposure on scrambles along the route and at the summit
Highest point	2,030 m (summit); 1,990 m (without the final scramble)

An ascent to the highest point in La Pedriza, involving some complicated route-finding and scrambling over granite boulders with few handholds. A chance to explore the wild and remote corners of the complex landscape of La Pedriza.

- The walk begins and ends at the car park at Canto Cochino. To find it, drive out from the centre of Manzanares el Real to the west and turn right where a signpost points to La Pedriza. This road will lead you to the visitor centre, and then on into the park of La Pedriza, climbing and then descending on a bendy road until about 1 kilometre from the edge of town you reach a large car park on the right, with two bar/restaurants (open at busy times).

- The last 2 kilometres of this walk follow the same route as part of Walk 26. I would have preferred to avoid this repetition, but most of the walk is very different, and the terrain is so complex that I have chosen this so as to give you a good chance of navigating the route. On this walk the descent is much easier than the ascent in terms of technical difficulty and route-finding.

- If you wish to explore the area of La Pedriza more fully, see the notes in the introductory section of this book.

- *At some weekends and in the summer months, vehicular entry to La Pedriza is limited, and therefore at busy times you should arrive early, as the barrier can be closed after 9.30 pm. No more than 270 vehicles are allowed in the park at the same time. Between October and June access is only limited at weekends between 10.30 and 1600 hours.*

- *If you arrive and cannot gain entry during the summer months, there is a free bus service from Manzanares el Real (Plaza de la Iglesia).*

- **The rocky area of La Pedriza is an absolute labyrinth, and it is easy to get lost. There are many ways to approach Las Torres. I have chosen this route because it is less complex than some others. The ascent follows the marked route 'PR-M1' and the descent follows 'PR-M2'. All of the 'PR' routes are marked with yellow and white paint, and you must follow the paint all the way. See the introduction section of this book for an explanation of how the paint symbols work.**

- Park at Canto Cochino *(1)*. Keeping the two bar/restaurants on your left, walk down the road towards the river, and go left to cross it on a bridge. You will see various paint marks on the bridge, because several marked routes cross here. At the far side of the bridge turn left. One path (the PR-M18) stays close to the river bank. But you should follow another path, further to the right, and heading north-west through the trees. At GPS waypoint *(2)* you will be on the right path. Ignore a minor path which goes off to the north at this point, and stay on the main path looking for paint at all times. This first part of the walk is easy going on a good path. At GPS waypoint *(3)* it goes a little to the right and starts to ascend easily.

- After a little less than 1 kilometre of this gentle ascent, you will reach a series of zigzags where the steepness increases considerably. At the top you will reach a level area, with a semi-clearing in the trees. This is Collado Cabron *(4)*, from where several routes depart. For this route your aim is to ascend the rocky ridge to the north. There is more than one way of getting there. Look for the officially marked footpath PR-M1, which is the first path to the left as you reach the Collado. Continue to follow the yellow and white paint, keeping a keen eye open for it all the time as you ascend. Waypoint *(5)* should confirm that you are on the correct path. The route crosses rocky areas with no obvious path, and involves some awkward scrambles, where if you are in a group you may be able to help each other.

- The path twists and turns, passing through areas of weirdly-shaped rocks many of which have local names, such as *La Vela* (the candle), *el Pajarito* (the little bird) and, above on the right at an altitude of 1,698 metres, Cerro del Diablo (Devil's Hill). You will then arrive at the col of Collao Romera, where the path goes through woodland to the right (east) and then downhill *(6)*. However, it quickly turns left to cross the eastern slopes of the Milanera ridge. You will now ascend steeply. In one or two places you may find a bolt or belay to help you up the rocks. Continue until you reach the top of the ridge *(7)*, where you can continue to the north-east until you reach a level area, the Collado del Miradero. Here another path comes up from the right *(8)*. Make a note of it, because it will be your descent route.

- From Collado del Miradero, the path continues along the ridge, just north of east, and reaches the summits of Las Torres *(9)* in only just over half a kilometre. You can scramble up the peaks if you are so inclined, but take care. Granite does not provide many handholds and the ascents, and more particularly the descents, can be tricky.

WALK NO. 27

- When you are ready to depart, return the way you came to Collado del Miradero, then turn left into a good path downhill to the south-east at first and then south. It is a marked path, officially the PR-M2. Follow it downhill, still on yellow and white paint. It swings to the left at an area called Los Llanos then swings right again. Continue downhill. At a crossroads of paths marked with four cairns (Cuatro Caminos) *(10)* go straight on. A little farther down you will pass a path going left near a stream. It goes up to La Ventana. Ignore it and keep straight on on the PR-M2.

- You will soon reach the valley bottom near the river. Not far to the left a wooden bridge leads to the Giner refuge, but to return directly to the start at Canto Cochino turn right as you reach the river path and follow it all the way back *(11)*. To the right of some buildings, cross another river on a bridge and a right turn leads to the car park.

APPROXIMATE GPS WAYPOINTS (UTM)

1	Start and finish	424373 4511330
2	On the path PR-M1	424401 4511606
3	Farther on the path	423755 4512282
4	Collado Cabron	424639 4512890
5	On the path PR-M1	424487 4513265
6	Downhill	424523 4513863
7	Ridge	424711 4514719
8	Collado del Miradero	425457 4515651
9	Las Torres	425977 4515725
10	Cuatro Caminos	425594 4514302
11	Turn right along river path	425391 4513002

Scrambling in La Pedriza - **WALK 27**

WALK NO. 28

WALK NO. 28 - HUECO DE SAN BLAS

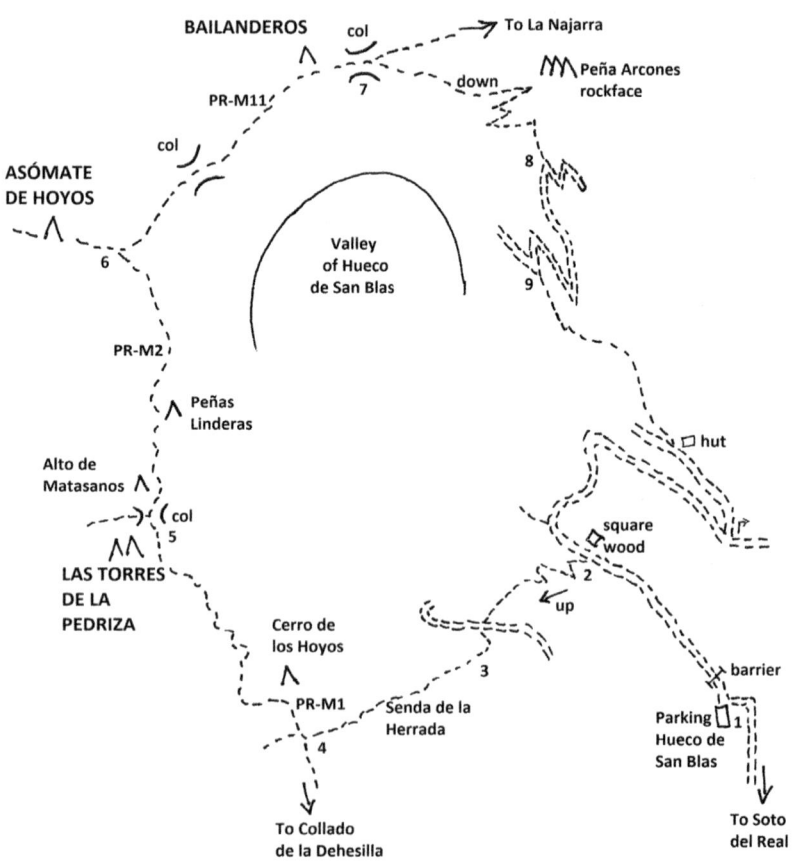

WALK NO. 28

HUECO DE SAN BLAS AND LA PEDRIZA

Distance	24 km
Ascent	1,370 metres
Overall grade	Strenuous
Terrain	Paths, boulders and some scrambling
Exposure	No real exposure, but there is scrambling and a squeeze under a rock
Highest point	Cuerda Larga: 2,219 metres

A varied and spectacular walk circling the valley of Hueco de San Blas, which includes scrambling over boulders while exploring the rocky labyrinth of the eastern section of La Pedriza, ascending to a couple of peaks on the Cuerda Larga and then returning to the valley next to the Peña Arcones rock face, which lies underneath the La Najarra peak.

Hueco de San Blas – also referred to on some maps as Hoya de San Blas – is an open valley to the east of La Pedriza, at the foot of the peaks on the Cuerda Larga. As it lies just outside the Guadarrama National Park, it suffers significantly less traffic than other nearby areas and is therefore an excellent starting point to explore the surrounding peaks. The closest village is Soto del Real, a 40-minute drive from Madrid.

- The walk starts from parking Hueco de San Blas *(1)*, a small car park accessible by dirt road from Soto del Real. The easiest way to get there is to take Avenida de España in Soto del Real until the surfaced street turns into a dirt road. Continue for 3 km – going straight at a cross roads and over a cattle grid – and take the first right turn after that. After approximately 1 km, take the first left onto the dirt road above the Palancares reservoir. After a further 2 km, you will cross a bridge and arrive at a small car park with information boards.

- Leaving the car park, walk up the wide track, past a barrier and gate. After 1.5 km, (and immediately as you arrive at a small, walled wood beyond the trees to your right), you will see a path to the left of the track *(2)*. Head up the path as it zigzags up through the forest. You will eventually reach a wide track above.

- Cross the track onto the path on the other side, which heads to the left before swinging around right. The path is fairly clear, but some cairns will start to appear where it's not. The path (known as Senda de la Herrada) winds a short way through the trees and, after 250 metres, bends right *(3)* and starts to climb, now in a straight line westward through the forest. After reaching some rocky viewpoints, Senda de la Herrada continues up the left-hand side of the forested gully, with the large craggy rock face of Cerro de los Hoyos on its other (northern) side.

- After 1.7 km of climbing up the gully, you will reach Collado de la Ventana (the Col of the Window) *(4)*, where white/yellow painted stripes signal the PR-M1, a circular route around La Pedriza. At Collado de la Ventana, the PR-M1 runs south to north; start following the white/yellow stripes to the right (north) towards the large semi-circular rock face of Cerro de los Hoyos.

- The route (I don't use the word path here as quite often there's no defined path; you just follow the white/yellow stripes as they lead you over boulders, through gullies, across the occasional clearing and through trees) will skirt around to the left and then up behind Cerro de los Hoyos, at which point you will have to do a bit of easy scrambling. The route then leads you under a rock. It's a tight-ish squeeze, but much better than the alternative of climbing over it. Still following the same markings upward, you will soon come face to face with La Esfinge (The Sphinx), a large rock formation with a very vague resemblance to its Egyptian counterpart. Indeed, it seems that every rock formation in La Pedriza has its own name, far too many to include here. Nevertheless, it's worth researching a few beforehand to make this section of the walk all the more rewarding.

- The route, at all times marked with the white/yellow painted stripes of the PR-M1, continues to wind its way upward through the rocky labyrinth and over boulders. Some more scrambling is required at times, although it's nothing over complicated, with scant exposure.

- Continue following the markings and you will finally reach Portacho (or Cancho) de los Gavilanes *(5)*, next to the jagged peaks of Las Torres (The Towers) – La Pedriza's highest point – which are to your left. You'll know you're there because, after a clearing with a circular man-made windbreak, you suddenly emerge from the rocky labyrinth and you're faced with a col (Collado de Matasanos) and the rocky outcrop of Alto de Matasanos ahead, with otherwise unrestricted views over mountain scrubland towards the ridge on the horizon to the north (the Cuerda Larga). Whereas the PR-M1 circuit swings left (west) behind Las Torres (peaks which are mentioned in Walk 27), you now leave that route, continuing straight (north) across the col of Matasanos on a path marked with cairns and occasional white/yellow marks of the PR-M2.

- This path climbs over Alto de Matasanos and then continues across mountain scrubland, skirting to the left of Peña Lindera, and ultimately heading towards the Cuerda Larga to the north. After 2.5 km of steady but gentle climb following the cairned and marked path, you will reach the Cuerda Larga *(6)*, and the wider path that runs along it from west to east. This path is marked with the white/yellow stripes of the PR-

M11 (however, as of the date of writing, an attempt had been made to replace paint with plastic or metal strips affixed to rocks, many of which had lost their respective colours, meaning that the path was marked by grey and silvery stripes...).

- Swing right (left would take you to the peak of Asómate de Hoyos), down the slope to the east, across the col of Collado de Pedro de los Lobos, and then up again, still on the same well-trodden path, over the rocky peak of Bailanderos. On the far side of Bailanderos, descend the path to the col between Bailanderos and La Najarra.

- Just as the path starts to level out on the col, look for the cairns that mark a path to the right (before you reach a cluster of rocks) *(7)*; although not too obvious at the beginning, the path becomes more evident as you go, and cairns lead the way. You will soon start descending through the pine forest to a series of viewpoints over Hueco de San Blas. At a couple of points the cairns disappear suddenly, in which case return to the last cairn and look to the trees to the left, where you will find a hidden path going through.

- Approximately 1 km after you left the col, you will emerge from the trees altogether and approach the large rock face of Peña Arcones, which lies just below the La Najarra refuge. The path slowly descends towards the bottom of the rock face until you arrive at a small section of scree. The cairns seem to disappear here, but drop down a few metres and you'll see that they continue below to the right, underneath the path you were just on.

- The cairns will take you on a few long zigzags. They disappear at times, but persevere as they are there and will lead you to the gully and stream (which you cross) that run vertically below Peña Arcones and ultimately to the large W-shaped track you can see below.

- Once you have reached the W-shaped track *(8)*, head down it. After 1 km, on what is the second sharp right-hand bend *(9)*, leave that track (straight) down a path that slowly descends in a straight line through the forest. Continue down this path for approximately 2 km until you reach a large track, next to a lookout post on the left.
- Here, swing left and continue for 800 metres until you reach another large track, crossing from left to right, with a signpost. Turn right, following the arrow to Arroyo Mediano. This track circles around the bottom of the valley and after 3.5 km, you will arrive back at the starting point.

APPROXIMATE GPS WAYPOINTS (UTM)

1	Car park	429974 4514857
2	Turn left onto path	429006 4515745
3	Head up Senda de la Herrada	428266 4515152
4	Collado de la Ventana	427101 4514694
5	Portacho de los Gavilanes	426091 4515786
6	Turn right onto PR-M11	425842 4517513
7	Turn right onto descending path	427938 4518509
8	W-shaped track	428861 4517798
9	Continue straight	428757 4517503

WALK NO. 29

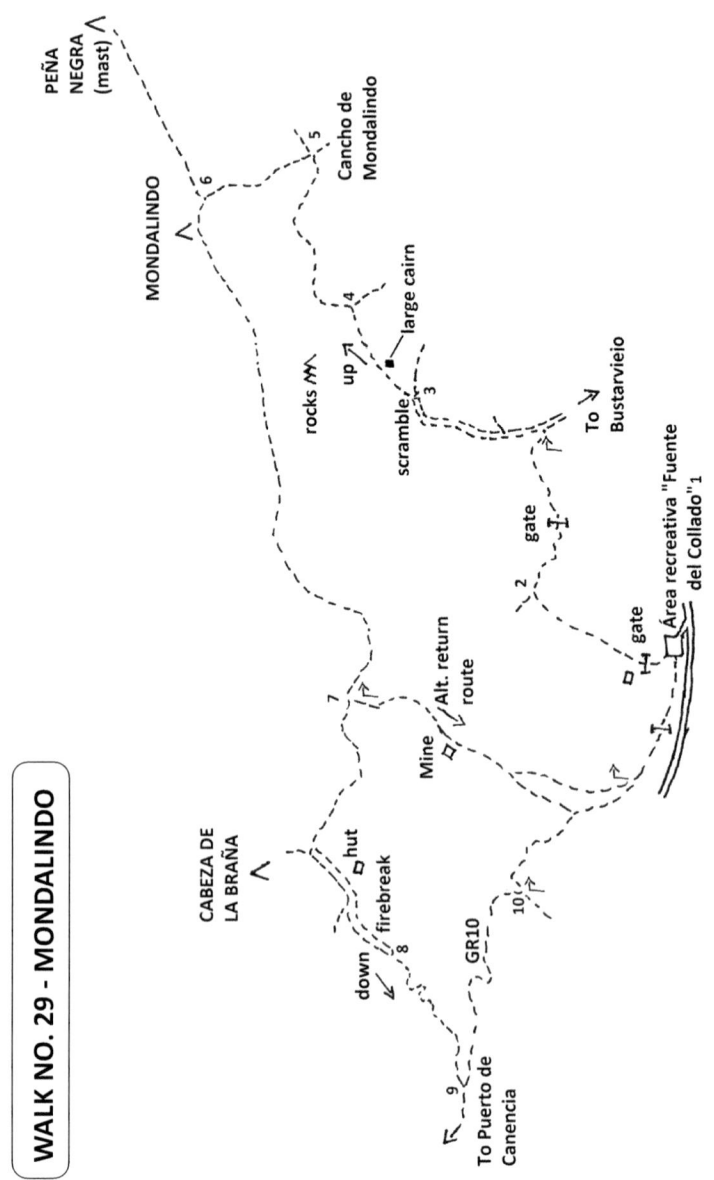

WALK NO. 29

MONDALINDO AND PEÑA NEGRA

Distance	21 km
Ascent	1,050 metres
Overall grade	Moderate
Terrain	Footpaths, tracks and some easy scrambling
Exposure	None
Highest point	1,854 metres

A walk to the rounded peaks of Mondalindo (also known as Cabeza de Cervunal) and Peña Negra at the eastern end of the Guadarrama range for views over the La Cabrera ridge, Montes Carpetanos and towards the Sierra de Ayllón.

- The walk starts in the Área Recreativa 'Fuente Del Collado' *(1)*, a parking and picnic area next to a football field, located to the left of the M-610 road just before you reach the village of Bustarviejo (from Miraflores). This should not be confused with Fuente del Collado restaurant, which is to the right of the road some 200 metres before the picnic area. From the car park, walk through the metal gate in the trees to the north-west. Head straight on, up the path, which quickly swings right through the trees (leaving the Depósito de Bustarviejo on your left).

- Continue along that path for approximately 1 km (ignore any tangents, especially a path to the right that hugs a wall as it swings away after you emerge from the trees). You will ascend a short section and soon arrive at a crossing with another, wider, path *(2)*. Turn right on the larger path in the direction of Bustarviejo. You will shortly come to a makeshift wire gate. Pass through it, making sure you close it behind you, and continue on until you reach a wider track crossing left to right, with signs indicating 'Paisaje Ganadero' and a wooden post with a red ring, indicating the Bustarviejo R2 local route.

- Turn left here up a large dirt track, away from the village. There are a few tangents on each side, but stay on the main track. About 500 metres later, you will see a post for a local route marking a path to the right and a post with an 'X' to the left. Ignore both and again, stay on the main track. The track starts to bend around to the right, and suddenly changes into a smaller, although clear, path that heads through some trees.

- As soon as the path emerges from the trees, the stone wall to your left bends away to the left towards some rocks *(3)*. Look along that wall and you will see a cairn. Follow the cairns on an easy scramble over the rocks and, when you emerge on top of them go on to the path on the other side. A large, symmetrical square cairn on a rock will confirm you are on the right path, which then swings upward to the left in the direction of a large rocky outcrop above you (north-east). Ignore any tangents to the left and right. The cairned path continues upward and skirts underneath the outcrop, eventually merging with the slightly larger path that ascends steeply from the south *(4)*. Follow that path left, upwards.

- The path climbs and starts to zigzag up and swings around the gully to your right, before eventually bending around left and levelling out onto the top of the sheer rock face of Cancho de Mondalindo that was on your right during the ascent. As it levels out completely you reach a plateau *(5)*, and you will see a post (for Bustarviejo R3 route) marking the visible track heading upwards left in a northerly direction; some rusty metal fence posts in front of you and a descending path beyond them, and a large set of rocks to your right – Cancho de Mondalindo – which are worth a visit for the views over the top of the rock face.

- From Cancho de Mondalindo, head upwards on the large northerly track with the marker post. The path from here has substantial loose rock and after about 1 km of ascent, you will reach a col *(6)* with another R3 route marker post and a fence crossing in front of you. Take the path heading to the right, which leads to Peña Negra, the peak you can see to the east with a mast. The path is marked with cairns, but you'll be heading for the mast at all times. You then return the same way to the last R3 marker post and follow the fence to the geodesic marker for the peak of Mondalindo, some 200 metres beyond the post.

- From Mondalindo, take the path along the fence towards a rain gauge (a rocket-like metal structure) and follow it downwards. The descent is initially steep, on loose rock, but it eventually levels out to undulating land. You can see the path that you'll be following as it heads off on the broad ridge into the distance, next to a fence. You will see occasional R3 marker posts along the way.

- After another gentle ascent and then descent, you will eventually arrive at a broad, open col (Collado Abierto) with an R3 marker post that points to the left *(7)*.

- *(To cut the walk short, follow the arrow and path to the left as it descends the hill, past the Torre de la Mina (Mine Tower), until you reach white/red GR10 markings on a large path at the bottom of the hill. Turn left and follow those markings back to the start.)*

- From the post, look up to the mast on Cabeza de la Braña, the hill in front of you to the north-west. You will see that there's a path that leads to the top, although you won't yet see where the path starts. To find it, cross the col next to the fence until you start to encounter dense bushes. Then swing left away from the fence and follow the line of the bushes until you find a path; this path starts climbing and swings around to the right, ultimately in the direction of the mast.

- After about 1 km of ascent (and before reaching the mast), you will meet the treeline, some cairns and a large firebreak to your left. Follow the firebreak left down the hill next to the fence (there's a viewpoint, a hut known as Mirador de Madrid, to the left of the firebreak as you descend). After 400 metres, ignore the gate and the track that heads into the trees to the right, and continue down the firebreak, hugging the fence and treeline on your right. Where the firebreak ends, follow the path straight ahead next to the fence *(8)*. It shortly emerges onto some rocks. Find the cairns among the rocks, which mark the steep and rocky descent of Cuesta de la Plata to the fields and stone wall that you will see below. Hands and bottoms may be needed at times, but the descent is not exposed.

- The lower you get and the less rocky the terrain, the more potential offshoots appear to the left; ignore them. If in doubt, you will ultimately be heading for the path along the wall that you can see below, so keep to the path that is most likely to get you there. When you reach that path, head along it in a southerly direction, keeping the wall to your right. After about 800 metres, you will see a rock with white/red stripes marking the GR10 trail; swing sharp left onto that large path *(9)*.

- Follow the GR10 path as it winds its way down the hill, marked with white/red stripes along the way. After about 2 km, you will come to a fork in the path, with a signpost indicating Camino del Pinar and Bustarviejo *(10)*. Follow the arrow left to Bustarviejo. Here the white/red marks are somewhat more intermittent, but continue to follow what has now become a large path, and then subsequently a dirt track. Ignore any large paths or tracks that head off to the left (which lead up to the Torre de la Mina).

- You will eventually arrive at a barrier across the track. The car park is about 500 metres beyond it.

APPROXIMATE GPS WAYPOINTS (UTM)

1	Área Recreativa Fuente del Collado	438841 4523025
2	Path right at crossing	439251 4523793
3	Turn left along wall up rocks	440451 4524434
4	Paths converge	440926 4524862
5	Cancho de Mondalindo plateau	441793 4525064
6	Turn off right to Peña Negra	441560 4525710
7	Post indicating alternative return route left	438655 4524888
8	Path continues straight along the fence	437106 4524633
9	Sharp left onto GR10	436353 4524236
10	Signpost, keep left to Bustarviejo	437497 4523883

WALK NO. 30 - PATONES DE ARRIBA TO CANCHO DE LA CABEZA

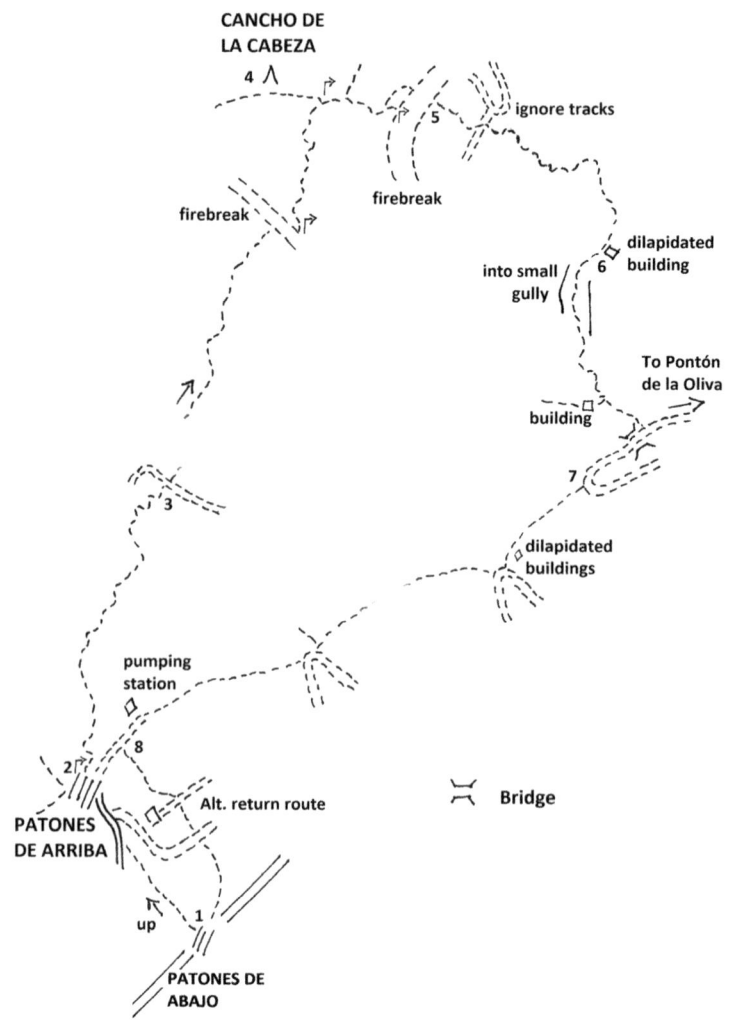

WALK NO. 30

PATONES DE ARRIBA TO CANCHO DE LA CABEZA

Distance	15 km
Ascent	910 metres
Overall grade	Moderate
Terrain	Tracks and footpaths
Exposure	None
Highest point	Cancho de la Cabeza: 1,264 metres

A walk through the medieval village of Patones de Arriba and up to Cancho de la Cabeza, with views over the El Atazar reservoir. There's also an option to extend the walk to visit Pontón de la Oliva, one of the first dams built to catch water for Madrid.

Patones de Arriba is a splendid village hidden in an enclave 60 km to the north-east of Madrid. It's a perfect example of *arquitectura negra*, or 'black' architecture, which uses dark slate as a building material and is common to the area. The village was rather unexpectedly proclaimed a kingdom unto itself in the 17th century – hence its other name Pequeño Reino de Patones (Small Kingdom of Patones); its mayor was the king, with a direct line to Charles III of Spain. Patones was subsequently abandoned for many years, but has recently been restored and is now a bustling village, with bars, restaurants, rural B & Bs and handicraft shops and stalls. It's extremely popular on weekends, so much so, that I would strongly advise against trying to drive up to the village except on weekdays as parking space is very limited. Instead, park in its sister village of Patones de Abajo, which is where this walk starts. However, the initial section of the walk can be avoided if you are able to drive up to Patones de Arriba. Whichever you decide, the village itself is the star of this walk and is worth spending some time exploring, either at the beginning or at the end of the walk; if you can book a meal or a night's stay there, even better.

- The walk starts in Patones de Abajo *(1)*. The main M-102 road from Torrelaguna runs through the middle of the village. Take the turn-off to Patones de Arriba and after 350 metres turn right, following the large P sign to a large dirt car park some 50 metres away.

- Start walking up the large path to the north-west, past an information board and a chain barrier, in the direction of the bridge/aqueduct you can see in the canyon. The path is clear and it climbs gradually up some steps under the bridge/aqueduct, eventually reaching a road. Walk up the road a short distance until you reach the village of Patones de Arriba.

- Make your way to the highest part of the village; as you climb past the Taberna Real restaurant, turn left onto Calle del Chopo and you will start to see white/red (GR300) and white/yellow (PR-M14) painted stripes and painted blue stickmen. The blue stickmen mark the Senda Genaro – a 70-km circular route that explores the area (if you've chosen to wander around the village first, you might also have seen similar markings or marker posts in the lower part along a river bed… ignore those as they mark another section of the Senda Genaro).

- A bit further along Calle del Chopo, you will see a wooden information board (number 7: *'Eras de Pizarra'*) and a post indicating the Senda Genaro and GR300/PR-M14 routes. Turn right there *(2)*, following the arrow on the post, onto a path that ascends out of the village through the slate-walled fields and buildings above it. You will eventually leave that behind and you will be in the midst of scrubland that is typical of this area. The path meanders around the hills at gradually increasing altitude.

- After 1.8 km from the village, you will arrive at a crossing of paths *(3)*. Ignore the options to the left and right and continue straight on. You will be accompanied at all times by the white/red/yellow markings of the GR300/PR-M14 and light-blue stickmen, as well as occasional wooden posts with the same information.

- After the path has descended and then climbed again for a couple of kilometres, you will arrive at a large firebreak. Turn right, and you will see another wooden post at the top, pointing left towards 'Poblado del Atazar'. Follow this path left for 600 metres as it climbs, until you reach another signpost, this time offering you the option of Cancho de la Cabeza to the left. Follow that arrow left for 100 metres to the top of the Cancho *(4)* for wonderful views over the reservoir and the mountains of Sierra de Ayllón lying to the west.

- From Cancho de la Cabeza, return to the last signpost, but now follow the arrow to Senda Genaro/GR300 Poblado del Atazar. After a further 200 metres, there's another sign. Continue to follow arrows to Poblado del Atazar, following the path marked with blue stickmen and white/red stripes, ignoring any tangents off to the right or left. You will very shortly reach a large firebreak; however, due to an almost-imperceptible fork in the path about 50 metres beforehand, you will encounter one of two scenarios: a) where you reach the firebreak, you may also find a signpost. If so, follow the arrow left towards Poblado del Atazar, and after 100 metres take a small path that leaves the firebreak to the right; or b) where you reach the firebreak there's no signpost, but you should be able to see the signpost up the firebreak to your right. In this case, cross the firebreak straight ahead onto the path on the other side *(5)*. This path, which is the same for both options a) and b), winds down the hill through the forest.

- After 500 metres, the path meets a bend in a larger track to the left and another track heading perpendicular to the right; ignore them both and continue downwards on the same footpath. That larger track on the left will be a constant presence as it winds down the hill alongside or below the path you're on; ignore it as it eventually connects to the road that you will also see intermittently on your left. Immediately after the point where that track finally meets the road you will come to a dilapidated slate building *(6)*. Here the path swings down right into a gully, and then left (south) along the bottom of it. Continue along the bottom of the gully for approximately 1 km and you eventually emerge from the trees at a stone bridge.

- *(From here, there's an option to extend the walk with a visit to Pontón de la Oliva. To do this, rather than cross the bridge right, turn left and head up the track until you meet the road. Carefully cross the road to a layby (called Parking Cerro de la Oliva). You have large tracks to the right (white/red stripes) and left (with a sign to Senda Presa de la Parra). Ignore both and take a path through the trees that starts directly between them. This path will take you into a gorge that swings around right to Pontón de la Oliva. Return the same way. This will add approximately 4 km to the walk.)*

- Turn right onto the track and cross the bridge, and then continue on the track for 500 metres until it makes a sharp left-hand bend *(7)*. However, don't take the bend, but continue straight ahead, now off the track, onto a path (past the small stone marker with the yellow and white/red crosses).

- The path runs straight, upwards at first and then descending, past some dilapidated buildings on the left, to a bend in a large track (in fact, it's the same track you were on earlier). Ignore the track and continue on the path on the other side of the bend. You will again climb and descend to a further bend in the track, which you also ignore. Instead, climb the path up the steep slope on the other side. As soon as the path starts to level out, it will start to slowly descend and will eventually change into a dark gravel track (at the Patones water pumping station). Patones de Arriba is a short distance down the track.

- Return to Patones de Abajo by retracing your steps and descending the road and gorge. Alternatively, for fabulous views over Patones de Arriba, from the dark gravel track and before reaching the first buildings in the village, swing left onto a path *(8)* that will take you to the top of the left-hand side of the gorge. From here, return the same way or continue over the top and down the other side on a number of paths that drop down to Patones de Abajo.

APPROXIMATE GPS WAYPOINTS (UTM)

1	Car park	458957 4523229
2	Path leaving Patones de Arriba	458418 4524070
3	Crossroads	458882 4525477
4	Cancho de la Cabeza	459531 4527351
5	Path off firebreak	460198 4527460
6	Swing right next to dilapidated building	461128 4526638
7	Continue straight at bend	461024 4525481
8	Start of alternative return to Patones de Abajo	458570 4524113

WALK NO. 31

WALK NO. 31 - LA CABRERA

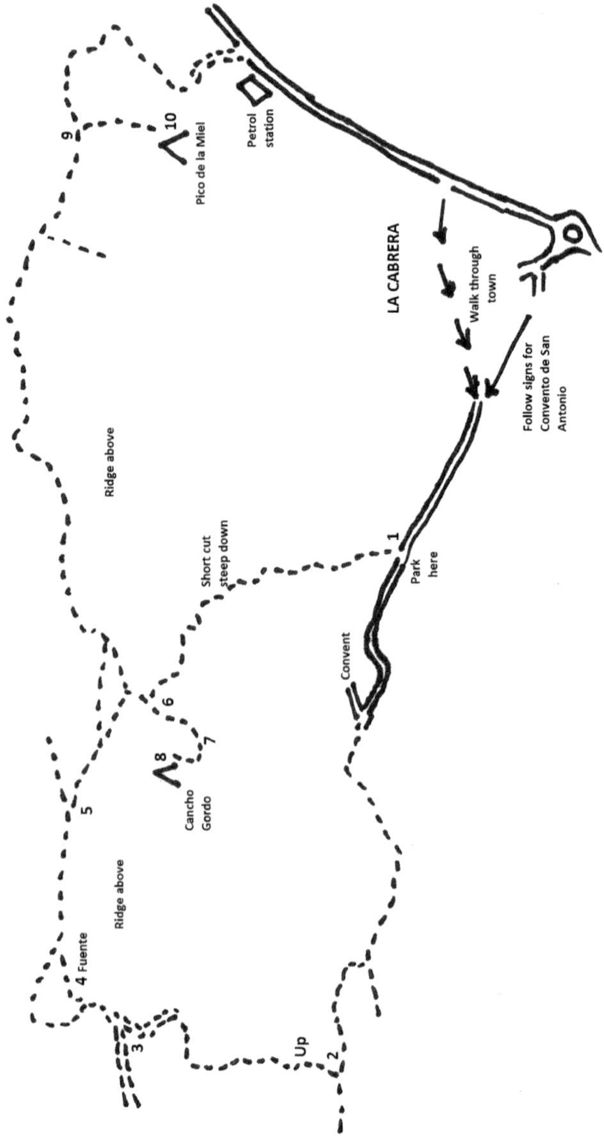

La Cabrera ridge - **WALK 31**

WALK NO. 31

LA CABRERA CIRCUIT

Distance	17 km
Ascent	650 metres
Overall grade	Moderate
Terrain	Surfaced track, footpaths and an optional short scramble
Exposure	A little at the very summit
Highest point	1,560 metres

A circuit through spectacular granite hills, ascending to the summit of a jagged ridge, but with exposure only at the very summit, which can be bypassed.

La Cabrera is a small town close to the A1 Madrid to Burgos motorway. Just to one side of the road is a landscape of jagged rocks, which makes a magnificent sight from the motorway. This walk makes a complete circuit of the southern and northern sides of the ridge, with an optional ascent to the summit, and a steep short cut for those who want a shorter day.

- Driving north from Madrid on the Burgos road, leave the A1 at junction 57 and enter the town of La Cabrera, still going north. Pass the Hotel Mavi on the right and go straight on at the roundabout. At the following roundabout turn left, and follow signs to *el Convento de San Antonio*. At a couple of minor junctions take the major of the roads and you should see more signs for the convent (which is open to the public at times – see below for information and times). If in doubt, ask somebody for the 'Calle Subida al Convento'.

- The road becomes a concrete track, ascending very slightly through open country with the rocky ridge above on the right. Look up there to identify a steep gully coming down from a breach in the top of the ridge. The optional short cut will come down it later in the day. When you are practically level with the gully there is a good place to park. There are some stone seats and a cross on the left, with good parking on sandy ground opposite *(1)*.

- Walk along the main track westerly on the road which becomes a broad dirt track. With the convent entrance to the right it swings left and becomes a footpath. There are paths going off at times both right and left, but stay on the main GR10 footpath, marked with red and white paint, but 2.5 kilometres from the start of the walk leave the GR10, and instead take a path uphill to the right *(2)*. Follow the path around several bends to the top of a crest and then, veering a little to the right, look out for a telephone mast. (I am referring to a local mast nearby, not a larger one on the top of a high hill much further to the north.) Go to the base of the small mast. The path swings round to the right of the antenna and then left. It becomes a broad track, and descends slightly to a junction with a large cairn where a track leads down to the left *(3)* to the village of Valdemanco. Ignore this left turn and instead turn right, uphill, now heading north-east. The path splits into two on more than one occasion, but the paths come back together again. There is a broken-down old *fuente* amongst the undergrowth *(4)*. Continue up the path which is now marked with yellow and white paint. It swings to the south as though to go up to a col, but then quickly veers back to the north. After a further 300 metres, the path veers to the right. The high part of the ridge is now above you on the right, as you head east below its northern slopes.

- About 2 kilometres from the Valdemanco track *(3)* the path forks *(5)*. Take the right fork, and then shortly afterwards at the next fork, take the right fork once more. This path leads you to the top of the steep gully which descends directly to the start of the walk. There is an enormous cairn marking the spot *(6)*. Shortly before the large cairn, look for some smaller cairns and a minor path on the right (west). It leads you towards the highest point of the ridge, Cancho Gordo. The path goes diagonally up to the left, and then swings to the right round the end of the hill before starting to descend on the other side. But just as the descent starts, leave the path and go up to the right *(7)* then scramble easily through a narrow rocky gap and into a meadow. Turn right into the meadow with the summit rocks on your right. A little farther on a cairn marks the start of an ascent up bare rock. It is an easy scramble to the summit *(8)* but a little exposed, so take care. At the summit you will find a ruined building and great views along the whole of the ridge. This is a great place for spotting griffon vultures which nest here in large numbers.

- From the summit, return the way you came to the large cairn at the top of the steep gully *(6)*.

- *If you wish to do a shorter walk, follow a steep and sandy path descending directly down the gully from the large cairn. It is sandy, loose and slippery at times, but it is a well-used route. In fact it can be heavily eroded. The path splits and then converges more than once. At the foot of the slope, a broader track leads ahead directly to the parking space at the start of the walk.*

- For the full circuit, at the large cairn take a minor path going to the north-east, on the northern side of the ridge. You will soon rejoin the main path marked with yellow and white paint. Go to the right (east and then north-east) along it. The path zigzags about but broadly speaking holds its contour. Below on your left you will have a good view over the plain leading down to Lozoyuela, and you should see a railway line in the distance. Continue on the path with the high ridge above to your right at all times. Ignore a path to the right going between two hills and keep to the left. Soon the path goes to the south-east and begins to descend. Ahead you will see the pointed rocky hill of Pico de la Miel (1,392 metres altitude) ahead. The main path swings left *(9)* before Pico de la Miel, but minor paths lead straight on to the base of the hill, which you can ascend over granite boulders without too much difficulty. There is no specific route. You need to find the best way for yourself. There is no serious exposure, but take care not to slip. There is a big drop to the far side of the summit *(10)*.

- From Pico de la Miel, return the way you came to join the yellow and white path and turn right along it going south-east. It zigzags and gets steeper, then swings down towards the motorway which you will soon see below. The path joins a dirt track on which you should turn right to descend towards the motorway. Stay on the track until it reaches a filling station and then walk south-west along the secondary road (not the motorway!) towards the village for about 0.75 kilometres (there is little traffic). Turn right as you see bars and shops in a side street, and look for the town hall, where there are at least two bars for refreshments. Continue on streets going slightly south-west, and then look for the road signposted for the Convento. Turn right along it to reach the car park within about 1 kilometre.

APPROXIMATE GPS REFERENCES (UTM):

1	Start and finish	446916 4524116
2	Turn right	444817 4524389
3	Track from Valdemanco	444739 4524940

WALK NO. 31

4	Fuente	444906 4525201
5	Fork right	445874 4525536
6	Top of gully	446304 4525268
7	Up to the right	446152 4525054
8	Summit	446105 4525099
9	Before Pico de la Miel	448623 4525712
10	Pico de la Miel	448738 4525509

THE CONVENT

Originated in the 11th century; restored in the 20th century.

Lived in by missionaries.

Open to visitors normally at 11:30, 12:00, 12:30, 17:00, 17:30, 18:00 (reduced hours in the winter)

Pico de la Miel - **WALK 31**